mein frankfurt und ich. portraits
my frankfurt and i. portraits

Rezensionsexemplar

mein frankfurt und ich.
portraits

my frankfurt and i.
portraits

SOCIETÄTS
VERLAG

© März 2011 – alle Rechte vorbehalten:
all rights reserved:

Herausgeber: Producer:	Trägerverein des Frankfurter Jugendrings e. V. Hansaallee 150 60320 Frankfurt am Main
Fotografien: Photos:	Anna Pekala
Redaktion: Editorial staff:	Christina Bender Sébastien Daudin Gudrun Ranftl Turgut Yüksel Judith Zimmermann
Übersetzung: Translation:	Sandra Ebuzoeme Silke Vaillant
Design: Layout:	Florian Albrecht-Schoeck Societäts-Verlag, Nicole Proba
Druck: Printed by:	Bercker Graphischer Betrieb GmbH, Kevelaer
Verlag: Publisher:	Societäts-Verlag Frankfurter Societäts-Medien GmbH Frankenallee 71 – 81 60327 Frankfurt am Main
ISBN	978-3-7973-1252-5

Aus Gründen der besseren Lesbarkeit wurde die männliche Sprachform in den Texten dieses Buchs verwendet. Selbstverständlich sind immer beide Geschlechter angesprochen.

Ein Projekt von:
A project by:

Inhalt

Grußwort — Seite 8
Oberbürgermeisterin der Stadt Frankfurt am Main – Petra Roth

Greeting — Page 9
Lady Mayor of Frankfurt am Main – Petra Roth

Vorwort — Seite 10
Vorsitzender des Frankfurter Jugendrings – Jan Lamprecht

Preface — Page 11
Chairman of the Frankfurter Jugendring – Jan Lamprecht

Über das Buch — Seite 12
Christina Bender, Sébastien Daudin, Gudrun Ranftl,
Turgut Yüksel, Judith Zimmermann

About this book — Page 15
Christina Bender, Sébastien Daudin, Gudrun Ranftl,
Turgut Yüksel, Judith Zimmermann

Frankfurt: Migration — Seite 18
Frankfurter Jugendring – Gudrun Ranftl

Frankfurt: Migration — Page 23
Frankfurter Jugendring – Gudrun Ranftl

50 Portraitaufnahmen — Seite 27
Fotografien: Anna Pekala
Interviews: Christina Bender, Sébastien Daudin, Gudrun Ranftl,
Turgut Yüksel, Judith Zimmermann

50 Portrait shots — Page 27

Photographs: Anna Pekala
Interviews: Christina Bender, Sébastien Daudin,
Gudrun Ranftl, Turgut Yüksel, Judith Zimmermann

Über die Fotografin Anna Pekala — Seite 128
About the photographer Anna Pekala — Page 129

Die Portraitierten und ihre Vereine — Seite 130
Portrayed people and their associations — Page 130

Danke — Seite 134
Frankfurter Jugendring – Jan Lamprecht, Turgut Yüksel
Acknowledgements — Page 135
Frankfurter Jugendring – Jan Lamprecht, Turgut Yüksel

Grußwort

Viele eindrucksvolle Fotografien finden sich in diesem Bildband „mein frankfurt und ich. | portraits" vereinigt. Sie stellen ein Bekenntnis zu Frankfurt als Heimat dar.

Dank ihrer fotografischen Qualität veranschaulichen diese Aufnahmen die verschiedenen individuellen Vorlieben; sie verdeutlichen das persönliche Suchen, den eigenen Ort zu finden und ihn den Mitmenschen durch das Auge der Fotografin zu vermitteln.

Dieser Bildband ergänzt die „Parade der Kulturen". Die „Parade der Kulturen" gehört zum Frankfurter Ereignis-Reigen wie die Fastnacht oder der Weihnachtsmarkt.

Frankfurt ist eine Stadt, in der Begegnungen gepflegt werden zwischen den Menschen aus unterschiedlichen Kulturen. Zugleich bestehen intensive Beziehungen von den hier lebenden Bürgern zu lauschigen oder lebendigen Ecken, Winkeln, Flecken und Lokalitäten. Denn Frankfurt ist eine Stadt mit Herz.

Für eine gemeinsame Identität unserer städtischen Gesellschaft sind wir auf den menschlichen Zusammenhalt und einen grundlegenden Konsens der verschiedenen Anschauungen und Lebensweisen angewiesen. Es geht uns stets um den Einzelnen wie um die Stadt. Wegen der Frankfurter Internationalität wird die Erde ein Dorf; überall haben wir in Frankfurt Nachbarn, die in alle Winkel der Welt enge persönliche Kontakte haben.

Die „Parade der Kulturen" ist ein Zeichen, uns anzustrengen, damit alle integriert werden. Dies verdeutlichen auch die Portraits. Diese Fotografien an ausgewählten Orten sind ein sichtbarer Ausdruck der jüngsten Umfrage des Bürgeramtes, Statistik und Wahlen, wonach 84 Prozent der Frankfurter gern in Frankfurt leben.

Ich wünsche allen bei der Betrachtung der Bilder, dass sie von der Lebensfreude der Frankfurter angeregt und angesteckt werden und dadurch eine Bereicherung für ihr eigenes Leben erfahren.

Petra Roth
Oberbürgermeisterin der Stadt Frankfurt am Main

Greeting

This illustrated book "my frankfurt and i. | Portraits" consists of many impressive photos. They are an expression of the subject's commitment to Frankfurt as their home.

Due to the portraits' photographic quality, these recordings visualize different individual preferences. They point out a personal search, to find one's own place. This is conveyed through the eye of the photographer.

This illustrated book complements the "Parade of Cultures". It is part of Frankfurt's annual events such as carnival or the Christmas Market.

In Frankfurt, encounters are valued with people from different cultures. At the same time there is an intensive relationship between the citizens living here and secluded or lively corners, niches, spots and locations, because Frankfurt is a city with heart.

We need to rely on human solidarity and essential consensus of different views and ways of living to achieve one identity within the community. It is always about each individual as much as about the city. Due to Frankfurt's internationality, the world becomes a village. For example, we have neighbours in Frankfurt that have close personal relationships all over the world.

The "Parade of Cultures" is setting an example to all of us to respect everybody. The portraits also visualize this. These photos at chosen locations are a visible expression of the latest citizen survey, statistics and elections. They state that 84 percent of Frankfurt's citizens enjoy living in Frankfurt.

I hope you feel inspired by the pictures and the Frankfurter's lust for life. May the experience enrich your own personal life.

Petra Roth
Lady Mayor of Frankfurt am Main

Vorwort

In Frankfurt leben viele Menschen aus unterschiedlichen Ländern und Kulturen zusammen. Diese Menschen prägen mit ihren kulturellen Einflüssen das alltägliche Leben in der Stadt. Frankfurts buntes und vielfältiges Gesicht spiegelt sich in Kindereinrichtungen, Schulen, Universitäten, am Arbeitsplatz, auf Sport- und Spielplätzen sowie in unzähligen Vereinen und Verbänden wider.

Dieses gemeinsame Leben ist ein hohes Gut.

Auf Dauer ist das friedliche vielfältige Zusammenleben keine Selbstverständlichkeit. Es muss immer wieder aktiv gelebt und gezeigt werden, und wir müssen weiter daran arbeiten, dass Ausgrenzung und Feindlichkeit gegenüber Menschen – egal, woher sie stammen und wie sie aussehen – in unserer Gesellschaft keinen Platz haben.

Und genau aus diesem Grund, um die Vielfalt Frankfurts an einem Tag zu demonstrieren, führt der Frankfurter Jugendring gemeinsam mit dem Amt für multikulturelle Angelegenheiten, der Kommunalen AusländerInnen-Vertretung und dem Jugendbildungswerk der Stadt Frankfurt sowie Sponsoren und privaten Unterstützern die „Parade der Kulturen" durch. Sie ist eine außergewöhnliche Form der Präsentation des Miteinanders in dieser unserer schönen Stadt und sie ist zugleich Ausdruck des toleranten, respektvollen Zusammenlebens.

Dieser Fotoband ist aus der „Parade der Kulturen" entstanden und soll sowohl über den Tag der Veranstaltung als auch weit über die Grenzen Frankfurts hinaus wirken.
Die Portraits machen die Verflechtung der in Frankfurt lebenden Kulturen mit ihrer Stadt deutlich sichtbar. Der Fotoband zeigt, wie sehr diese Menschen mit ihrem Alltag und ihrem Engagement in Frankfurt verankert sind, und er zeigt auch, dass wir als Frankfurter stolz sein können auf unser friedliches Miteinander der Kulturen.

Entdecken Sie 50 Frankfurter an besonderen Plätzen in dieser Stadt und lernen Sie die Vielfalt Frankfurts aus einem neuen Blickwinkel kennen!

Jan Lamprecht
Vorsitzender des Frankfurter Jugendrings

Preface

In Frankfurt, many people live together from different countries and cultures. These people shape the daily life of the city with their cultural influence. Frankfurt's colourful and versatile face is reflected in children's facilities, schools, universities, at workplaces, at leisure and sport facilities and playgrounds as well as uncountable clubs and associations.

These conjoined cultures are highly valued.

The peaceful multifaceted coexistence is not a matter of course. It needs to be actively re-lived and demonstrated repeatedly. We need to keep working on it. Exclusion and hostility towards humans – regardless of their heritage and their appearance – have no place in our community.

The "Parade of Cultures" is held by the Frankfurter Jugendring together with the Department for Multicultural Affairs, the Communal Foreigner Agency and the Jugendbildungswerk Frankfurt as well as sponsors and private supporters to show Frankfurt's diversity on one day. It is an unusual form to demonstrate togetherness in this our beautiful town. At the same time, it is the expression of tolerant and respectful community living.

This volume of photographs evolved from the "Parade of Cultures". It should extend the parade past the day of the event and far beyond the boundaries of Frankfurt.
The portraits make the complexity of the different cultures living in Frankfurt visible. The volume of photographs shows how much these people are grounded with their daily lives in Frankfurt. They demonstrate their commitment within their city. It points out as well that Frankfurt's citizens can be proud of their peaceful diverse community.

Discover 50 of Frankfurt's citizens at chosen locations and get to know Frankfurt's diversity from a new perspective.

Jan Lamprecht
Chairman of the Frankfurter Jugendring

Über dieses Buch

Sie kennen das vielleicht: Sie treffen Ihre Berliner Freunde in der Hauptstadt wieder und Sie werden gefragt, wie Sie denn in Frankfurt nun klar kämen. Gut, wunderbar, antworten Sie und ernten ungläubiges Staunen. Sie versuchen zu erklären und schließlich landen Sie beim fast trotzig dahin geworfenen Satz:
Und Frankfurt ist außerdem so wunderbar bunt!

Es ist nicht immer ratsam, diesen Satz auszusprechen. Allzu leicht setzt man sich dem Vorwurf aus, zu denen zu gehören, die naiv an Multikulti festhielten und die Probleme der Einwanderungsgesellschaft verleugneten, um ihr Bild der heilen Welt vor Rissen zu bewahren. Es scheint aus der Mode geraten zu sein, sich an Vielfalt und Buntheit zu erfreuen. Sorgenfalten und Skepsis wirken souveräner.

Dieses Buch will keine Politik machen. Aber dieses Buch entsteht zu einer Zeit, die von reißerischen Schlagzeilen in den Zeitungen über Migranten und deren Analysten birst sowie von vergifteten Debatten und von Reflexen des Unbehagens auf allen Seiten.
Und daher ist dieses Buch zwangsläufig politisch.
Es ist ein Bekenntnis.
Es ist das Bekenntnis, dass wir uns freuen, in Frankfurt mit vielen verschiedenen Kulturen zusammenzuleben.

Ein Bekenntnis ist auch die alljährliche „Parade der Kulturen" in Frankfurt, die die Vielfalt der Frankfurter in einem Demo-Umzug vor Augen führt. Bei der Vorbereitung der Parade 2010 kam in uns der Wunsch auf, dass es dieses einmalige Ereignis verdient, weiter ausgedehnt zu werden, und zwar auf die restlichen Tage im Jahr und auch auf all die Stadtviertel und Straßen, durch welche die Parade an einem einzigen Tag nicht ziehen kann: Ein Buch, das den bunten Umzug fortführt und verlängert, und in dem einige Teilnehmer außerhalb des Schritttempos der Parade mehr von sich zeigen und erzählen können. So lauteten die Grundüberlegungen, als wir uns das erste Mal zusammensetzten, um abzuwägen, ob sich die Idee denn überhaupt umsetzen lassen würde. Nach einigen Monaten Arbeit an dem Projekt haben andere Inhalte an Wichtigkeit gewonnen:

Es geht uns nicht mehr allein um Vielfalt. Denn das hieße, die Menschen, die hier abgebildet werden, wieder zu einem Kollektiv zusammenzufassen. Nein, es geht uns hier um den Einzelnen. Es ist der Einzelne, der sich hat fotografieren lassen, an seinem Ort, in der Kleidung seiner Wahl. Es ist der Einzelne, der sich uns in Gesprächen geöffnet und uns seine ganz individuelle Geschichte erzählt hat.

Während der Fotoaufnahmen wurden wir stille Zeugen eines erstaunlichen Prozesses: Eine Glocke von Konzentration legte sich über die Fotografin und ihr Modell, eine Glocke, die uns Außenstehenden den Zutritt verwehrte und sich aus der Umgebung herauslöste. Es war nicht mehr die Vertreterin Mexikos, die sich in einer Apfelweinkneipe fotografieren ließ, um den Gegensatz Mexiko-Deutschland plakativ zu demonstrieren. Es geschah etwas anderes: Unter der Glocke eignete sich das Modell diesen Ort an, und es entstand ein neuer Raum. Und vielleicht ist dies die Grundformel von Migration: Zwei Strömungen, Kulturen, Geschichten stoßen aufeinander und es entsteht etwas Neues.

Wir mussten viel nachdenken über unseren Begriff von Migration. Über eigene Vorurteile, Empfindlichkeiten, eigene, nie mit der Realität abgeglichene Wunschvorstellungen und über teilweise eigenes Unwissen. Zuerst erschien es den meisten von uns als selbstverständlich, dass sich alle Portraitierten in ihrer jeweiligen Landestracht fotografieren lassen würden. Daraufhin widersprach Turgut heftig. Warum sollte sich der Türke als Bergbewohner verkleiden, wenn er doch auch in seiner Herkunftsstadt Jeans und T-Shirt trägt? Ob Deutsche mit einer „urdeutschen" Herkunft denn vielleicht bereit wären, sich mit Dirndl und Lederhosen fotografieren zu lassen? Ob das Teil unserer Identität sei? Nein – erwischt. Und doch brauchte dieses Buch ein Konzept. Wir haben uns schließlich darauf geeinigt, es den Modellen selbst zu überlassen und unseren Wunsch als Bitte zu formulieren. Niemand sollte sich verkleidet in eine folkloristische Schablone gepresst fühlen.

Eine weitere Herausforderung war die Benennung der Nationalität. Wie ist das mit der Spanierin, die in Deutschland geboren wurde – müssen wir da Deutschland als Land hinzufügen? Was ist generell mit all denen, die deutscher Nationalität sind? Was, wenn die Eltern aus unterschiedlichen Ländern kommen und der Portraitierte in Deutschland geboren ist? Der Versuch, alles ganz korrekt und transparent zu benennen, scheiterte an der Vielfalt und Einzigartigkeit der verschiedenen Lebensgeschichten.

Fest steht, dass in unserem Buch 50 Portraits von Frankfurtern sind, die sich an ihrer Stadt erfreuen, auch wenn sie manchmal mit ihr hadern. Es sind Menschen, die sich in Vereinen und Verbänden engagieren, um sich einzumischen und sich in das Stadtleben einbringen zu können. Es sind Menschen, die Frankfurt durch ihr Tun bereichern.

Jede Begegnung mit diesen Menschen eröffnete auch uns ein kleines Universum: Es waren nicht nur die Geschichten über Herkunft und große Reisen, die schließlich nach Frankfurt führten, die uns überraschten, uns rührten und beeindruckten, sondern es waren auch die Erzählungen über die Orte, die sich die Menschen ausgesucht hatten: Einige davon waren uns bis dahin gänzlich unbekannt gewesen. Andere lernten wir mit den Augen der Portraitierten und durch ihre Geschichten neu kennen.

Leider konnten wir die verschiedenen Erzählungen nicht in Gänze ausformuliert in das Buch aufnehmen – dann wäre es kein Bildband, sondern ein ganz anderes Buch geworden. Ihre Neugier als Betrachter und Leser wird nicht immer befriedigt werden können. Aber wir hoffen, jedes einzelne Foto wird Ihnen dennoch einen Ausschnitt einer Lebensgeschichte erzählen und einen ganz besonderen Blick auf Frankfurt zeigen.

Wir wünschen Ihnen viel Freude beim Entdecken.

Christina Bender, Sébastien Daudin, Gudrun Ranftl,
Turgut Yüksel, Judith Zimmermann

About this book

You may have experienced something similar: You catch up with your Berlin friends in the capital. They ask you how you are getting on in Frankfurt now. Fine, terrific, is your answer. They give you disbelieving looks. You try to explain and finally you end up with a statement such as: Besides, Frankfurt is so incredible colourful!

Caution with this kind of statement. You risk branding yourself as having a naive belief in the benefits of a multicultural society and a disregard for some of the broad difficulties of migration. As if you are trying to hold on to a perfect image of the world and preserve it from being damaged. It seems as if it has become out of fashion to enjoy diversity and colourfulness. Worry lines and skepticism appear to be more popular.

This book is not about politics. However, this book arises during a time of lurid headlines in the newspapers concerning migrants and their analysts. On all pages, poisoned debates evoke uneasiness.
Therefore, this book is inevitably political.
It is a commitment.
It is the commitment to be excited about living together with various different cultures in Frankfurt.

We are also committed to the annual "Parade of Cultures" in Frankfurt. It visualizes the diversity of Frankfurt's citizens in one event. When organizing the 2010 parade we felt it deserved more. We desired to expand this unique event to the remaining days of the year and to all the city quarters and streets that the parade does not march through: "A book that carries on the colourful parade and extends it. Where participants have the opportunity outside the walking pace of the parade to express themselves further and talk about their lives." Those were the grounds when we sat together contemplating if the idea was achievable at all. While working on the project, other subjects gained importance:

We are no longer only concerned about diversity. Because this would mean the people who are going to be pictured here are going to be combined as a collective again. No, we care about the individual.
It is about the portrayed individual at his favorite location wearing his clothes of choice. Hence, it was the individual, who opened up to us by telling his very own story.

During the photo session, we were silent witnesses of an astonishing process: A cap of concentration lay over the photographer and her object. A cap that did not grant us, the outsiders, access. It distinguished itself from the surroundings. It was no longer the pictured Mexican representative at a cider bar who demonstrated the strong contrast between Mexico and Germany. Something else happened: Under the cap, the object adopted the surroundings and a new location evolved. Maybe this is the basic format for migration: Two streams, cultures, stories come across each other and something new comes into existence.

We had to think a lot about our notion of migration. About our own prejudices, sensibilities, own imaginations that we never aligned with reality and partially about our own ignorance. At first most of us presumed that all people taking part would want to wear their individual national gowns when being photographed. Thereupon Turgut disagreed fiercely. Why should a Turk get dressed up as a mountain dweller especially if he wore jeans and T-shirt in Turkey as well? Germans, will they be happy to be portrayed wearing a "typical" German dirndl and leather pants? Is this part of our identity? No – there you go! However, this book needed a concept. We finally agreed to let the individuals decide for themselves. We put our wish forward as a polite request. Nobody should feel forced to dress up to resemble a folkloristic image.

A further difficulty proved to be the naming of the nationalities. How about the Spaniard who was born in Germany – do we need to add Germany as a country? Generally speaking what about all those whose nationality is German? What if the parents are from different countries and the person portrayed was born in Germany? The attempt at being precise with naming and keeping it transparent failed due to the diversity and uniqueness of the various backgrounds of the individuals involved.

One thing is for certain, our book consists of 50 portraits of Frankfurt's citizens who enjoy their town even if they quarrel with it as well sometimes. They are people who are devoted members of clubs and organizations. They are very involved and integrated into city life. They are people who enrich Frankfurt through their actions.

Every time we met with these people, it also opened up a little universe for us: It was not only about the stories of origin and far travels that led to Frankfurt, which surprised, amazed and stirred us. Also the stories about the places where they chose to be portrayed: Some of them were totally unknown to us. Others we got to know through the eyes of the portrayed person and their story linked to it.

Unfortunately, we were not able to include the different stories in full lengths within this book – it would not have ended up being an illustrated book, but rather something else. Your curiosity as an outsider and reader will not always be satisfied. However, we hope that each photo gives you an impression of a cutout of someone's life story and conveys a very special view of Frankfurt.

We hope you enjoy the journey.

Christina Bender, Sébastien Daudin, Gudrun Ranftl,
Turgut Yüksel, Judith Zimmermann

Frankfurt: Migration

Geboren in Frankfurt, die Mutter aus Italien, der Vater ein Argentinier und selbst im Besitz eines deutschen Passes – das ist im 21. Jahrhundert nichts Ungewöhnliches mehr. Wollte man Menschen jeweils nur einem bestimmten Land zuordnen, käme man hier schnell an Grenzen; eine differenziertere Betrachtung ist erforderlich. Und dennoch: Die Kultur der Familie – entweder eines oder beider Elternteile – spielt auch heute noch eine wichtige Rolle im Hinblick auf die eigene Identität. Bei manchen Menschen bleibt der sehr enge Bezug zu einem Herkunftsland bestehen, andere wiederum übernehmen mehr aus der neuen Heimat. Es hängt natürlich auch davon ab, was die Menschen letztendlich dazu bewogen hat, nach Frankfurt zu emigrieren.

(M)EINE HEIMAT
Jedem Menschen, der einmal ein Land verlassen hat – aus welchem Grund auch immer –, wohnt eine Verbundenheit zu mehr als einem Land inne. Das erlebten wir immer wieder in den Gesprächen bei den Fototerminen zu diesem Buch. So erzählte uns Nasim Ghadimi, die als Kind aus dem Iran flüchten musste: So sehr sie auch als Kind den Iran abgelehnt habe, sei das Iranische immer ein Teil von ihr geblieben. Rhodora Schorr von den Philippinen beteuerte, ihr Herz sei stets zwischen zwei Ländern geteilt und Halil Özdemir bezeichnet mittlerweile die Türkei und Deutschland als seine beiden Heimaten.

WARUM FRANKFURT?
Große Migrationsbewegungen sind oft wirtschaftlich, politisch oder religiös begründet. Einreisegeschichten heute basieren außerdem auch noch oftmals auf individuellen Entschlüssen und unterscheiden sich von Mensch zu Mensch. Emilia Flügel aus Malaysia, die in unserem Buch portraitiert wird, kam zum Beispiel der Liebe wegen nach Frankfurt. Ranto Harilala Schlosser aus Madagaskar hat sich aus beruflichen Gründen zwischen China und Deutschland letztendlich für Frankfurt entschieden. Leider ist es bei einigen immer noch eine erzwungene Flucht aus ihrem Land, aber der eine oder andere bleibt auch in Frankfurt, weil ihm die Stadt und das weltoffene Flair von Beginn an gut gefallen haben.

RÜCKBLICK
Frankfurter mit einer langjährigen Tradition sind seit jeher rar, denn selbst die deutschen Bewohner der Stadt sind mehrheitlich aus dem Umland, aus anderen Städten Deutschlands und aus dem Ausland zugewandert. Noch im 16. Jahrhundert lebten sogenannte Permissionisten in der Stadt, Geduldete für eine begrenzte Zeit. Zu ihnen zählten Dorfbewohner, Bürger, Beisassen,

Juden und als größte Gruppen der Fremden in Frankfurt: Handwerksgesellen und Gesinde. Sie galten als Gemeinschaft minderen Rechts und waren zum Beispiel von der städtischen Armen- und Krankenfürsorge ausgeschlossen. Sie konnten nicht in den Rat gewählt werden und hatten auf das politische Geschehen keinen Einfluss. Der Status eines Frankfurter Bürgers konnte vor 1871 ausschließlich vererbt und nur in Ausnahmen durch Ehelichung erworben werden. Ein Aufstieg in das Frankfurter Stadtpatriziat, der nur wenigen gelang.

16. JAHRHUNDERT – IM NAMEN GOTTES

Eine erste große Fluchtwelle aus ganz Europa löste die Reformation aus. Entgegen des Wunsches von Papst und Frankfurter Bürgerrat, setzten die Bewohner Frankfurts im Jahr 1536 den Anschluss an das protestantische Bündnis durch. Flüchtende Protestanten wurden freundschaftlich aufgenommen und Frankfurt erwarb sich innerhalb Europas den Ruf, eine weltoffene Stadt zu sein. Aber nur kurze Zeit nach der ersten großen Einwanderungswelle regte sich bereits erster Widerstand gegen die Glaubensflüchtlinge. Immerhin wohnten Ende des 16. Jahrhunderts etwa 4.000 Flüchtlinge aus den Niederlanden bei einer Gesamtbevölkerungszahl von 17.000 in der Stadt. Flüchtende flämische und wallonische Exilanten wurden von den Frankfurter Bürgern nicht mehr so freundlich aufgenommen. Als Antwerpen in spanische Hände fiel, flüchteten noch mehr Niederländer – diesmal Angehörige der Oberschicht – von Antwerpen nach Frankfurt. Einerseits förderte dies den Aufschwung der Messestadt, die Frankfurter Börse wurde gegründet und die Stadt florierte aufgrund der hohen Steuereinnahmen, andererseits keimte der Neid auf, denn die neuen Bewohner waren den Frankfurtern handwerklich überlegen. Immer mehr Handwerker mussten sich als Lohnabhängige bei den Migranten verdingen, was große Ablehnung gegenüber den Fremden geschürt hat.

17. JAHRHUNDERT – UNERWÜNSCHT

1685 hob König Ludwig XIV. in Frankreich das Toleranzabkommen – das Edikt von Nantes – zwischen Katholiken und Protestanten auf. Eine neuerliche Flüchtlingswelle wurde ausgelöst. Von den insgesamt 200.000 Menschen, die ihr Land zurücklassen mussten, kamen etliche nach Frankfurt. Obwohl die Frankfurter Bürger die neuen Migranten alles andere als freundlich empfingen, blieben diese. Erst ein speziell auferlegtes Gottesdienstverbot und eine zusätzliche Abgrenzung bei der Aufnahme als Frankfurter Bürger hatten zur Folge, dass viele Calvinisten in die Städte rund um Frankfurt zogen, wie etwa nach Hanau, Friedrichsdorf und nach Neu-Isenburg.

JUDEN IN FRANKFURT

Von 200 Juden im 13. Jahrhundert stieg die Zahl auf etwa 26.000 Juden im Jahr 1910. Es gab mehrere Zuwanderungswellen, obgleich von jeher eine antijüdische Stimmung unter der

Frankfurter Bevölkerung herrschte. Im Jahr 1241 fielen Frankfurter Juden der sogenannten Judenschlacht zum Opfer, obwohl ein kaiserlicher Schutzbrief den Juden besonderen Schutz gewähren sollte. Immer wieder kam es zu Morden und Vertreibungen der Juden. 1462 entstand im Osten der Stadt – zum einen zur Beruhigung der Situation und zum anderen als Ausgrenzung – das erste Zwangsghetto für Juden, die Judengasse. Es entwickelte sich ein autonomes Leben innerhalb der Mauern, wobei Juden politisch ohne Rechte und mit nur sehr eingeschränkten Gewerberechten leben mussten. 1614 kam es, als eines der letzten Pogrome vor den Nationalsozialisten, zum sogenannten „Fettmilchaufstand", einem Überfall auf das Ghetto und zur zeitweiligen Vertreibung fast aller Juden. Später verbesserte sich die Situation der Juden zwar, wenngleich sie weiterhin nur eingeschränkte Rechte besaßen. 1796 löste Frankfurt das Judenghetto auf. Seit 1864 wurden die Rechte der Juden denen der Frankfurter gleichgestellt, und sie konnten sich in das politische, wirtschaftliche und gesellschaftliche Leben Frankfurts einbringen. Das nahm ab 1933 jedoch ein jähes Ende. Die Entrechtung und Vernichtung jüdischer Mitbürger wurden von den Frankfurtern nicht nur ohne großen Widerstand hingenommen, sondern auch selbst betrieben.

Ein ähnliches Schicksal von Zwangsansiedlung und der Ermordung durch die Nationalsozialisten betraf auch die Minderheiten Sinti und Roma.

18. UND 19. JAHRHUNDERT
Wirtschaftlich florierende Zeiten führten in Frankfurt immer wieder dazu, Fremde erst einmal willkommen zu heißen. Die Einreisewelle italienischer Händler bewirkte im 18. Jahrhundert einen wirtschaftlichen Schub für die Messe- und Handelsstadt. In ökonomisch schwierigen Zeiten jedoch versuchte man, die „Gäste" wieder loszuwerden.

Eine wesentliche Veränderung erfuhr Frankfurt im Jahr 1871, als das Gemeindebürgerrecht durch das deutsche Staatsbürgerrecht ersetzt wurde. Frankfurter war ab sofort jeder, der sich als Deutscher in Frankfurt dauerhaft niederließ.

ZUWANDERUNGSWELLEN NACH 1945
- Bis 1961 Flüchtlinge und Vertriebene aus dem Osten (etwa 12 Millionen aus der UdSSR, Polen, Rumänien, Ungarn, Jugoslawien, Tschechoslowakei);
- Seit Beginn der 60er Jahre Arbeits-Migranten aus Südeuropa (nach den Italienern folgten Arbeitskräfte aus Spanien und Griechenland und später aus der Türkei, Marokko und Jugoslawien);
- Ab den 70er Jahren zogen zu den mittlerweile dauerhaft eingewanderten Arbeitskräften auch

deren Familienangehörige nach. Zu dieser Zeit gab es bei etwa 70 Prozent der Migranten nur fünf unterschiedliche Herkunftsländer;
- Seit den 80er Jahren kam es aufgrund der weltweiten Krisen, der Auflösung des Ostblocks und des Balkankriegs zu einer komplexen Einwanderungswelle.

GEGENWART UND AUSBLICK

Die neuen Bewohner brachten und bringen Schätze aus einer anderen Welt und Erfahrungen aus zwei und mehr Ländern nach Frankfurt am Main. Der geschichtliche Rückblick zeigt, dass dies seit jeher eher kontrovers von Frankfurter Bürgern und der Stadt aufgenommen worden ist. Hat zu Beginn von Einreisewellen nicht selten ein wirtschaftlicher Nutzen für die Stadt im Vordergrund gestanden, gab es eine große Bereitschaft der Bürger dieser Stadt, Flüchtlinge aufzunehmen. Sobald sich jedoch die wirtschaftliche Situation verschlechterte, waren Ablehnung und Ausgrenzung der neuen Mitbürger die Folgen.

Und dennoch: Frankfurt hat sich mit etwa 40 Prozent der Gesamtbevölkerungszahl an Einwohnern mit Migrationshintergrund an der Spitze aller deutschen Städte positioniert. Rund 170 unterschiedliche Nationen leben in der Stadt in einem Dialog. Vielen gefällt das weltoffene Flair. Das friedliche Miteinander ist zu einem großen Teil den zahlreichen Frankfurter Vereinen, Institutionen und Gruppen zu verdanken. Sie engagieren sich für einen aktiven interkulturellen Austausch – vielfach wirken sie ehrenamtlich in dem Bereich integrativer Jugendarbeit, pflegen Kulturen der früheren Heimat und präsentieren diese in zahlreichen Veranstaltungen den Bürgern der Stadt. Es kommt zu einem Austausch von Kulturen und Erfahrungen. Sie helfen den neuen Bürgern in Deutschland anzukommen, sich in der Stadt einzufinden und wohlzufühlen. Darüber hinaus wirken städtische Institutionen und Religionsgemeinschaften sowie Sport- und Wohlfahrtsverbände seit Jahrzehnten in eben diesen Bereichen unterstützend. Aber auch Aufklärungsarbeit bei den deutschen Bürgern ist ein wesentliches Anliegen aller Initiativen. Die Integration ist über die Parteigrenzen hinaus ein wichtiger Bereich bei der Gestaltung der kommunalpolitischen Ziele und Aufgaben. So wurde 1990 das deutschlandweit erste Amt für multikulturelle Angelegenheiten (AmkA) gegründet. Das neue Amt der Stadt Frankfurt wird zum Vorzeigeamt und die Stadt Frankfurt beschreitet immer wieder neue Wege.

Viele Bewohner Frankfurts sind stolz auf das für Deutschland ungewöhnlich internationale Flair und sie lieben den unglaublichen Weltenschatz in ihrer eher kleinen Stadt. Frankfurter, Besucher und Touristen genießen den Luxus des reichhaltigen Angebots von Kunst, Kultur und nicht zuletzt das kulinarische Angebot aus den unterschiedlichen Ländern. Mit dem Ansatz, nicht immer gegen sondern für etwas zu demonstrieren, wird im Jahr 2003 erstmals die „Parade der Kulturen" durchgeführt. „Wir wollten mit der Parade die wunderschöne Seite der Vielfalt der Kulturen zeigen und erlebbar machen", so Turgut Yüksel, Mitinitiator der Parade der Kulturen und Referent im Frankfurter Jugendring, dem Veranstalter. Bei dem mittlerweile größten Frankfurter Fest engagieren sich tausende Menschen aus Vereinen und Institutionen, die im Jugend-, Migrations- und Kulturbereich ehrenamtlich tätig sind, und alle Einnahmen fließen direkt in Migrations-, Kultur- und Jugendarbeit – es ist ein einzigartiges Projekt.

Die Geschichte der Migration zeigt, wie sich Umstände und Bedingungen verändern. Es bedeutet einen ständigen Prozess von Begegnungen, von Herausforderungen aber zugleich auch von Chancen und Bereicherung. Es liegt an jedem Einzelnen, sich diesem spannenden Weg gegenüber zu öffnen, sich neugierig auf eine Reise zu begeben. Und jeder kann das direkt und mitten in Frankfurt am Main tun!

Gudrun Ranftl

Frankfurt: Migration

In the 21st century it is quite common for someone born in Frankfurt to hold a German passport even though their mother is Italian and the father is Argentinean. Nowadays, if you are trying to relate a person to only one country it is almost impossible. A more sophisticated view is essential. However, the family's culture, either of one or both parents, is still important today for your own identity. Some people keep a very strong bond with a country of origin. In turn, others relate more to their new home country. Another crucial point is the ultimate reason why people migrated to Frankfurt.

MY / A HOMELAND
Every human who has left a country for whatever reason will always feel they belong to more than one country. This is what we kept on experiencing during conversations at the photo shoots for this book. Nasim Ghadimi who had to take refuge from Iran as a child told us: As much as she rejected Iran as a child, the Iranian culture will always be a part of her. Rhodora Schorr from the Philippines assured us that her heart will always be divided between two countries. Halil Özdemir now describes Turkey and Germany to be both his home countries.

WHY FRANKFURT?
Major migration movements are often due to economic, political or religious reasons. Today's immigration reports are often based on each individual's decisions and vary from one person to another. Emilia Flügel from Malaysia, portrayed in our book, came to Frankfurt out of love. Ranto Harilala Schlosser from Madagascar had to decide between China and Germany for a career path and finally chose Frankfurt. Sadly, many people still experience a forced escape from their country. Still one or the other person remains in Frankfurt, because they have fallen in love right from the start with the city's world openness.

REVIEW
Seldom may you find citizens of Frankfurt that keep a true long lasting tradition. Even though, predominantly Germans immigrated from surrounding areas, other German cities and from abroad to Frankfurt. In the 16th century, "Permissionisten" were living in the city; suffering people who had the permission to reside for a certain period. These included amongst others villagers, citizens, prisoners, Jews and being the biggest group of 'strangers' in Frankfurt: journeymen and menial staff. They were a community with lesser rights than normal citizens. They were excluded from civic poverty and health care benefits, for example. They had no rights to

campaign and had no influence in politics of any kind. The status of a Frankfurt citizen could exclusively be inhabited until 1871 or acquired through marriage. A rise into Frankfurt's city council, which only a few achieved.

16th CENTURY – IN THE NAME OF GOD

All over Europe, the first major wave of migration led to reformation. In 1536, against the Pope's wishes and those of Frankfurt's citizen council, Frankfurt's citizens succeeded in the accession of the protestant alliance. Protestants who tried to escape were well accommodated and Frankfurt was soon known as a cosmopolitan city within Europe. Shortly after the first rush of migrants, resistance started stirring against the religious refugees. After all, by the end of the 16th century about 4.000 refugees from the Netherlands were residing in the city compared to an overall population of 17.000. Frankfurt's citizens did not welcome amongst others Flemish and Wallonian refugees living in exile anymore. When Antwerp fell into the hands of Spain, more Dutchmen fled. This time they were members of the upper class who fled from Antwerp to Frankfurt. On the one hand, it stimulated economic recovery in the trade fare city; Frankfurt's stock exchange was founded and the city flourished due to its high tax incomes. On the other hand, envy aroused because of the much better skilled new habitants. More and more craftsmen were taken on as wage earners by these migrants which led to rejection towards the strangers.

17th CENTURY – UNWANTED

In 1685, King Louis XIV abrogated the tolerance agreement in France – Edict of Nantes – between Catholics and Protestants. A further wave of refugees was released. A total of 200.000 people had to leave their country behind and several of them came to Frankfurt. Despite their possible prejudice, Frankfurt's citizens gave the new migrants a warm welcome, and many stayed. Not until a particular church service restraint and an additional differentiation at the intake of becoming a Frankfurt citizen did the Calvinists move to suburban areas like Hanau, Friedrichsdorf and Neu-Isenburg.

JEWS IN FRANKFURT

In the 13th century, there resided about 200 Jews in the city. By 1910, the number went up to about 26.000 Jews. There were several immigration waves, although ever since there has been an anti-Jewish vibe amongst the population of Frankfurt. In 1241, Frankfurt Jews fell victim to the so-called Jews' battle. Even though, a royal councilor's writ of protection failed to grant special safety. Repeatedly Jews were murdered and expelled. In 1462, the first constrained ghetto came into being in the Eastern part of the city, the Judengasse (Jews' Alley), in order to ease the situation and to segregate them. A self-governed life evolved within those boundaries. Jews had to cope without political rights and very limited commercial laws. In 1614, it came to one of the last pogroms before National Socialists the so-called "Fettmilchaufstand" (Fatty Milk Riot), an attack on the ghetto and banishment of almost all Jews temporarily.

Later the situation for the Jews got better indeed, even though they still had limited rights. In 1796, Frankfurt eliminated the Jews' ghetto. Since 1864, Jews' rights were on equal terms with Frankfurter's so they were able to integrate themselves into Frankfurt's political, economic and social life. This came to a sudden end from 1933 onwards. Frankfurt's citizens tolerated the deprivation of Jewish rights and carried out killings of Jewish citizens without any great resistance.

A similar destiny of forced settlement and killings by National Socialists experienced the minorities Sinti and Roma.

18th AND 19th CENTURY

Flourishing economical times repeatedly led to welcome strangers in Frankfurt. In the 18th century, an entry flow of Italian tradesmen caused an economic boost in the trade fair city. However, at difficult times the emphasis was to get rid of those visitors.

Frankfurt experienced a fundamental change in 1871. The council civil right replaced the German civil right. This meant that a German who resided in Frankfurt permanently was from now on a Frankfurter citizen.

IMMIGRATION FLOW PAST 1945

- Until 1961 refugees and people living in exile from the East (about 12 million from the USSR, Poland, Rumania, Hungary, Yugoslavia, the Czech Republic);
- Early 60s: labour migrants from South Europe (following the Italians was a workforce from Spain and Greece and later on from Turkey, Morocco and Yugoslavia);
- From the 70s onwards family members of those permanently immigrated workers followed. At that moment in time 70 percent of migrants came only from five different home countries;
- Since the 80s, there has been an extensive flow of immigration due to international crisis, resolution of the Eastern bloc and the Balkan War.

PRESENT AND FORECAST

The new inhabitants brought and still bring treasures from a different world to Frankfurt am Main, as well as their experience and knowledge from two and more countries. The historic review shows that ever since Frankfurt's citizens and the city itself accepted this rather controversially. At the beginning of an immigration flow, the city's economic benefit was at the foreground. This led to the citizens' great openness to admit refugees. As soon as the economic climate worsened, it resulted in rejection and exclusion of the new fellow citizens.

Yet 40 percent of Frankfurt's entire population has an immigrant background, which makes it the leading German city. People from about 170 different nations live together in the city in one dialog. Most people like the world open flair. A broad range of Frankfurt's clubs, institutions and communities are mainly accountable for the peaceful togetherness. They are committed to an active intercultural exchange. Frequently they contribute voluntarily in the areas of integrated youth work. Furthermore, they keep cultures of former home countries alive and represent those to the citizens at numerous events in the city. This leads to an exchange of cultures and experiences. They support new citizens on arrival, to settle down well in the city and to feel welcomed. Beyond that for decades, civic institutions and religious communities as well as sports and welfare organizations contribute supportively in these areas. To all the initiatives educational work amongst the German citizens is very important as well. Outside the party lines, a fundamental area of local political aims and tasks is 'integration'. Founded in 1990 was the first German-wide department for multicultural affairs (AmkA) in Frankfurt, which has become a flagship department. Again and again, Frankfurt keeps pursuing new ways.

Many of Frankfurt's citizens are proud of the city's international flair that is quite uncommon for Germany. They love the incredible diversity within their rather small town. Frankfurt's citizens, visitors and tourists enjoy the luxurious rich variety of art, culture and not least the choice of culinary cuisine from different countries. In 2003, the "Parade of Cultures" was held for the first time with the approach not to demonstrate against something, but rather for something. "With the parade we wanted to show the beautiful side of the cultures' diversity and make them come alive", Turgut Yüksel, co-founder of the Parade of Cultures and head of division of Frankfurter Jugendring, the organizer. It is the biggest event in Frankfurt by far now where thousands of people get involved from clubs and institutions. They work voluntarily in the areas of youth, migration and culture. All takings go straight to migration, culture and youth work – it is a project of its kind.

The history of migration shows how circumstances and conditions change. It means there is a constant process of encounters, challenges as well as chances and personal gains. It is down to each individual to open up to this exciting path, to be curious and go onto an unexpected journey. Everybody can do this in the middle of Frankfurt am Main!

Gudrun Ranftl

50 Portraitaufnahmen in Frankfurt am Main
50 Portrait shots at Frankfurt am Main

Emilia Flügel

Malaysia | Messe

Hochzeitspaare in Malaysia werden als „König und Königin des Tages" bezeichnet. Emilia Flügel zeigt sich im prunkvollen Hochzeitsgewand, dem Kebaya Songket. Wenn sie spricht, bewegen sich die Spiralen ihres Kopfschmucks und geben metallene Geräusche von sich.

„Die Messe mit ihren hohen Gebäuden ist ein guter Ort. Du weißt, du befindest dich definitiv in Frankfurt und nicht vielleicht in Malaysia oder sonst wo auf der Welt."

Malaysia | Messe (exhibition centre)

In Malaysia bride and groom are called "king and queen of the day". Emilia Flügel presents herself in a magnificent wedding gown, the Kebaya Songket. When she is talking the spirals of her headdress are moving and are giving off metallic sounds. "The exhibition centre with its high rising buildings is a good place. You know for sure that you are in Frankfurt and not maybe in Malaysia or elsewhere in the world."

Jean Jules Tatchouop

Kamerun | Riederwald

Auf dem Abenteuerspielplatz Riederwald hat Jean Jules Tatchouop schon seit jeher die Geburtstage seiner Kinder gefeiert. Seine Kleidung hat mit seinem Beruf zu tun, der spirituellen Kunst. „Ich mag die Ausstrahlung dieses Waldes. Das passt zu meinem Lebensstil – ganz ohne Druck und Hektik. Es ist für mich ein heiliger Ort, wo Kinder toben können. Ein echter Kinderort."

Cameroon | Riederwald

Jean Jules Tatchouop has always celebrated his children's birthday at the adventure playground in Riederwald. His clothes have something to do with his profession, with spiritual art. "I like the atmosphere of this forest. It fits my lifestyle – without any pressure or rush. It's a holy place for me where my children can romp about. It's a genuine children's place."

Monika Banasova

Slowakei | Campus Bockenheim
Monika Banasova hat gerade ihr Studium beendet. Sie trägt die traditionelle Tracht ihrer Heimatstadt Preschau.
„Während meines Studiums habe ich mich auf dem Campus in den Pausen gerne im Cafe KOZ aufgehalten. Hier gibt es ein Flair von Freiheit und studentischer Revolte, wohingegen sonst in Frankfurt alles eher geradlinig ist."

Slowakia | Campus Bockenheim
Monika Banasova has just finished her studies. She wears her hometown Preschau's traditional costume. "While I was studying I loved to spend my breaks in our student café, "Café KOZ". It has this special atmosphere of freedom and student's revolt at the same time, whereas the rest of Frankfurt is rather straight."

Georgina Mercedés Reyes

Dominikanische Republik | Ostend
„Als ich 1990 nach Frankfurt kam, ging ich oft in die Großmarkthalle, um Gemüse und Obst für große Veranstaltungen zu kaufen. Der Ort erinnert mich an den kleinen Markt, den mein Vater in meiner Heimat betrieb. Heute ist die Großmarkthalle eine Baustelle und wartet darauf, die neue Europäische Zentralbank zu werden. Dieser Schwebezustand zwischen Alt und Neu, Nicht-Mehr und Noch-Nicht gefällt mir."

Dominican Republic | Ostend
"When I came to Frankfurt in 1990 I often went to the wholesale market hall to buy vegetables and fruits for big events. The place reminds me of the local market my father used to run back home. Today, this market hall here in Frankfurt is a building site waiting to be transformed into the new European Central Bank. This transitory state between old and new, not anymore and not yet appeals to me."

Ismat El-Turk und Usama Sabih

Jordanien und Irak | Irakischer Friseursalon, Innenstadt
Nur auf den ersten Blick sehen die Gewänder von Ismat El-Turk und Usama Sabih sehr ähnlich aus, aber dann bemerkt man die unterschiedlichen Farben und Muster der Kopfbedeckungen. In Jordanien nennt man sie Hatda und im Irak Jeschmach.
„Wir sind hier bei meinem Friseur. Alle Iraker kennen ihn, nur mein Freund ist zum ersten Mal hier. Aber er ist ja auch Jordanier. Hier treffen wir uns mit Freunden und gehen dann um die Ecke essen. Wenn ein Iraker ein Geschäft hat, zum Beispiel ein Restaurant, geht man auch hin, wenn man keinen Hunger hat, nur um ihm beizustehen."

Jordan and Iraq | Iraqi hairdresser, City Centre
"Only at first sight the robes of Ismat El-Turk und Usama Sabih look very much alike. Then you notice the different colours and patterns of their headgear. In Jordan they are called Hatda, in Iraq Jeschmach. "We are here at my hairdresser's. Every Iraqi knows him except my friend who is here for the first time. That's because he is Jordanian. We meet our friends here and then we have something to eat just around the corner. When an Iraqi has a business such as a restaurant for example, you also go there if you are not hungry just to support him."

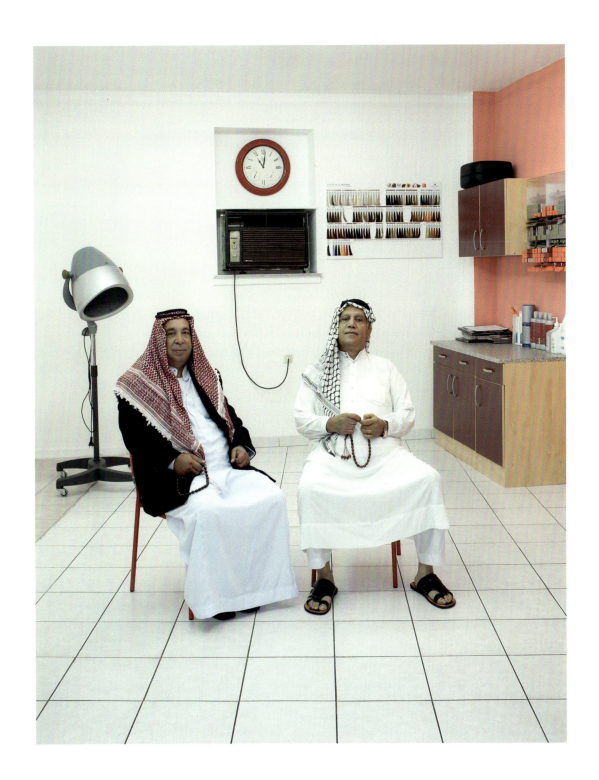

Mariam Mwabasi

Kenia | Günthersburgpark
Die 9-jährige Mariam hat sich den Günthersburgpark ausgesucht. „Ich war schon mal mit der Schule hier. Der Park ist so schön. Man kann mit dem Wasser spielen, toben und überall gibt es Blumen."

Kenya | Günthersburgpark
9-year-old Mariam has chosen Günthersburgpark. "I know the place from a school trip. The park is so nice. You can play with water, romp around and there are flowers everywhere."

Elsa Nava Villarroel

Bolivien | Bethmannpark
Elsa Nava Villarroel trägt ein Jagdkostüm aus dem Gebiet des Amazonas' Boliviens im Chinesischen Garten des Bethmannparks. „Hier habe ich mitten in der Stadt eine versteckte Ecke gefunden, um Ruhe zu finden und für mich sein zu können. Man hat das Gefühl, etwas näher an der Natur zu sein und man hört das Plätschern des Wassers – ein Kontrast zur Stadt."

Bolivia | Bethmannpark
Elsa Nava Villarroel wears a hunting dress from Bolivia, from the Amazon area. She had her photo taken in the Chinese garden in Bethmannpark. "I have found a hidden corner here in the middle of the city where I can relax and be by myself. You feel a little closer to nature and can hear the dabble of the water – a contrast to the city."

Grigorios Zarcadas

Griechenland | Innenstadt

Vom Gastarbeiter zum Rentner. Grigorios Zarcadas' Geschichte ist die der Zuwanderung. Mehr als die Hälfte seines Lebens verbrachte er in Frankfurt – ein echter Frankfurter Grieche. „Frankfurt bedeutet für mich mein Studium, meine Familie, mein Beruf, mein politisches und gewerkschaftliches Engagement – auch in der Griechischen Gemeinde. So wie Odysseus immer in sein Reich Ithaka zurückwollte, so zieht dennoch meine Sehnsucht hin zu Mutter Erde, die mich geboren hat. Dort möchte ich meine letzte Ruhe finden."

Greece | City Centre

From guest worker to senior citizen. Grigorios Zarcadas' story is about migration. He has spent more than half his life in Frankfurt – he definitely is a real Frankfurt Greek. "Frankfurt means a lot to me: I went to university here, founded my family, had my profession, was politically active as well as very committed to the union and also to the Greek community. However, just like Ulyssis always returned to his hometown Ithaka, I long for the place where mother earth gave birth to me. That's where I want to be buried."

Nino Kambegashvili

Georgien | Ostend
„Das Hotel Central, in dem das Foto entstanden ist, hieß früher Hotel Tiflis und hatte einen georgischen Besitzer, der es liebevoll mit Gegenständen und Bildern aus seiner Heimat dekorierte. Ich entdeckte es zufällig und verliebte mich auf Anhieb in diesen Ort! Der jetzige Besitzer hat das Interieur beibehalten. Die Hotellobby ist eine ideale Kulisse für meine Tracht, die früher von Männern getragen wurde, die in den Krieg zogen."

Georgian Republic | Ostend
"This hotel, where the photo was taken, is called Hotel Central now, but it used to be called Hotel Tiflis. The owner was from Georgia and he had it decorated lovingly with all kinds of objects and pictures from his home country. I discovered this place by pure chance and instantly fell in love with it! The new owner has kept the interior and the lobby is an ideal backdrop for my traditional gown. In the past it was worn by men who went to war."

Giovanni Belenzano

Italien | Niedereschbach

„Als ich 1984 nach Frankfurt kam, habe ich ganz in der Nähe der Großgärtnerei Niedereschbach gewohnt. Hier gibt es Pflanzen, an die ich mich erinnere als ich noch Kind war. Pflanzen, die es bei mir zu Hause gab, in meinem Dorf. Außerdem kann man Gipsfiguren kaufen für den Garten – wie in Italien."

Italy | Niedereschbach

"When I came to Frankfurt in 1984 I lived next to the Niedereschbach market garden. They have plants that remind me of my childhood. Plants, we had at home, in our village. You can also get sculptures for your garden – just like in Italy."

Fabiana Jarma

Argentinien | Ostend

„Ich finde die Naxoshalle richtig gut. Das ist so ein Schatz! So etwas braucht Frankfurt."

Fabiana Jarma ist eine temperamentvolle Argentinierin mit einer großen Leidenschaft für den argentinischen Tango – auch in Bezug auf ihre Alltagskleidung.

„Ich trage gerne Tangostil: Enge Röcke mit Schlitz, oftmals in schwarzer Farbe und natürlich Schuhe mit hohen Absätzen – Hauptsache sexy."

Argentina | Ostend

"I really like the Naxoshalle. That's a real treasure! Frankfurt needs such places." Fabiana Jarma is a lively Argentinian who loves the tango passionately. This is also reflected in her everyday clothes. "I love to wear tango style: tight-fitting skirts with a slit, often in black and high heels, of course – the main thing is to look sexy."

Halil Özdemir

Türkei | Auf dem Main

„Ich suche oft das Mainufer zum Radfahren auf, zum Flanieren oder einfach, um in die entspannten Gesichter der Menschen zu schauen. Vor 19 Jahren folgte ich meiner Frau nach Frankfurt und fing hier ganz neu an. Frankfurt ist mir mittlerweile so ans Herz gewachsen, dass ich jetzt zwei Heimaten habe. Was mir hier fehlt? Das Meer! Aber die Schiffe auf dem Main sind ein ganz guter Ersatz."

Turkey | On the river Main

I often go to the waterfront to ride my bike or go for a stroll or simply look into the relaxed faces of the people. 19 years ago, I followed my wife to Frankfurt and started from scratch. I have become so attached to Frankfurt since then that I now have two homes. What I miss? The sea! But the ships on the river make up for it quite well."

Ho-Jeong Reinbacher

Südkorea | Höchst

„Die Schule ist sehr hässlich, aber hier unterrichte ich unsere Kultur: Sprache, Tanz und Musik. Da dachte ich: Das passt. In Frankfurt gibt es viele Orte, die ich besonders mag, wie zum Beispiel den Botanischen Garten, den Flughafen und natürlich den Main. Ich bin auf einer Insel aufgewachsen und liebe das Wasser. Die Sehnsucht verlässt dich nie, deshalb ist jetzt auch meine Mutter zurück nach Korea gegangen."

South Korea | Höchst

"This school building is very ugly indeed, but I teach our culture here: language, dance and music. So I thought: that fits. There are many places in Frankfurt that I like, such as the Botanic Garden, the airport and the river Main, of course. I grew up on an island and love water. There is a constant yearning. That's the reason why my mother went back to Korea."

Bertrand Caradec

Frankreich | Hauptbahnhof
„Anfangs war ich einfach neugierig auf das Akkordeon. Heute ist es wie ein alter Freund, dem ich manchmal sehr nahe bin." Bertrand Caradec macht in seiner Freizeit keltische und bretonische Musik. Für ihn ist der Frankfurter Hauptbahnhof der beeindruckendste Deutschlands und ein Ort, der lebt und pulsiert.

France | Main Station
"Initially I was simply curious about the accordion. Today it is like an old friend who I am sometimes very close to." Bertrand Caradec plays Celtic music in his free time. For him the Main Station in Frankfurt is the most impressive place in Germany. It is a bustling, lively place.

Sandra Jiliana Peña Burgos

Kolumbien | Eckenheim
„Ich habe einen Ort gesucht, der zu meiner kolumbianischen Tracht passt: Er sollte prächtig sein, ein bisschen verwunschen und grün und auch einen Hauch konservativ. Das passt zu dem Traditionsbewusstsein meiner Kultur. Hier auf dem Hauptfriedhof gibt es all dies: verzauberte Orte, Blumen und Bäume, alte Mauern und Gebäude."

Colombia | Eckenheim
"I was looking for a place which fits my Colombian costume: it should be magnificent, a little enchanted and green and at the same time slightly conservative. A place that matches this sense of tradition in my culture. Here at Hauptfriedhof (main cemetery) you find all of that: enchanted places, flowers and trees, old walls and buildings."

Abderrahim Bouzaidi

Marokko | Hausen

„Die Moschee ist für mich ein Ort des Alltags, nicht der außergewöhnlichen Festtage. Es ist ein Ort der Reinheit und der Spiritualität – kurz: der Nähe zu Gott. Für mich ist die Moschee aber auch ein Ort der Bildung, an dem ich viel über meinen Glauben und über das Leben lerne."

Marokko | Hausen

"The mosque is part of my daily life and not just for the occasional bank holiday. It's a place of purity and spirituality – briefly – a place close to God. The mosque is also a place of knowledge where I learn a lot about my faith and life as such."

Ranto Harilala Schlosser

Madagaskar | Ostbahnhof

Ranto Harilala Schlosser fährt täglich auf dem Weg zur Arbeit hier vorbei.

„Mir gefällt die Abwechslung am Ostbahnhof. Hier steigen viele Menschen aus und ein. Zeitweise ist es sehr voll und hektisch und dann wieder vollkommen ruhig. Ein pulsierendes urbanes Leben kenne ich auch aus Tana, meiner Millionenstadt in Madagaskar. Nur Personenzüge fahren dort keine."

Madagascar | Ostbahnhof

Every day Ranto Harilala Schlosser comes past this place on her way to work. "I like the bit of variety here at Ostbahnhof. Many people get on and off trains. At times it is really crowded and hectic and then again completely calm. I am familiar with the bustling of urban life from Tana, the megacity in Madagascar I come from. The only difference is that there are no passenger trains."

Constanta Danilovic

Rumänien | Gutleut

Constanta Danilovic hat sich den Westhafen ausgesucht, weil er in unmittelbarer Nähe zu ihrer Wohnung liegt. Sie wollte nicht mit dem Folklorekostüm durch die ganze Stadt laufen.
„Den Hafen in Frankfurt mag ich. In Rumänien haben wir auch direkt am Fluss gelebt – an der Donau."

Romania | Gutleut

Constanta Danilovic has chosen the Westhafen (West harbour) because it is very close to where she lives. She didn't feel like walking through the whole city with her traditional dress. "I like the harbour in Frankfurt. In Romania we also used to live right next to the river – the Danube."

Agassi Bangura

Sierra Leone | Sachsenhausen

Agassi Bangura sitzt in seinem Atelier in der Städelschule, die er seit 2005 besucht. Hier verbringt er ganze Nächte mit Arbeit zwischen Kisten, Fotos und Materialien und kann seiner Kreativität freien Lauf lassen.

„Durch meine Kunst behalte ich die Bindung zu meinem Land. Meine Performance als Schamane zieht immer neugierige und belustigte Blicke an. Die Reaktion der Leute ist toll."

Sierra Leone | Sachsenhausen

Agassi Bangura is sitting in his studio at his art school, the Städelschule, which he has been attending since 2005. He spends whole nights here working with boxes, photos and all kinds of other materials. Nothing restricts his creativity here. "Through my art I keep in touch with my country. Whenever I do my Shaman performance, I attract curious and amused looks. The people's reaction is great."

Sunny Graff

U.S.A., Ohio | Westend

Sunny Graff macht seit fast 40 Jahren Taekwondo und wurde bereits in der Taekwondo Hall of Fame, New York, für ihr Lebenswerk geehrt. In der Sporthalle der Philipp-Holzmann-Schule in Frankfurt organisiert sie Kampfkunst-Lehrgänge und Workshops. „Sport ist mein Leben! Diese Halle ist eine der wenigen großen in der Stadt. Außerdem gibt es genügend Parkplätze. Das ist für alle praktisch und für meine amerikanischen Gäste sehr wichtig."

U.S.A., Ohio | Westend

Sunny Graff has been exercising taekwondo for almost 40 years and has already been honoured in the Taekwondo Hall of Fame in New York for her life's work. She organises martial arts courses and workshops in Frankfurt at the Philipp-Holzmann-Schule. "Sport is my life! This gymnasium is one of the few big gyms in the city. Besides, there is enough parking space. This is useful for everyone and very important for my American guests."

Tyagita Hidayat
und Mahar Muhammad

Indonesien, Java | Westbahnhof
Mahar Muhammad hat sich einen Hochzeitsanzug geliehen und Tyagita Hidayats Kleid wird beim Tanz der Blumenprinzessin getragen.
Muhammad: „Ich habe in Indonesien Germanistik studiert und viel über Goethe und Schiller gelernt. Jetzt kann ich ins Goethehaus gehen. Etwas, dass ich nur aus einem Buch kannte. Es ist wie ein Traum! Wir sind in unserer traditionellen Kleidung durch die Straßen gelaufen und waren so stolz."
Hidayat: „Mir gefallen die unterschiedlichen Gebäude – die alten und die modernen – ich mag die Gegensätze hier besonders."

Indonesia, Java | Westbahnhof
Mahar Muhammad has borrowed a wedding suit and Tyagita Hidayats' dress is usually worn for the Dance of the Flower Princess.
Muhammad: "I studied German in Indonesia and have learned lots about Goethe and Schiller. Now I can go to the Goethehaus, a place I only knew from a book. It's like a dream come true! We walked through the streets in our traditional clothes and were really proud." Hidayat: "I like the different kinds of buildings here – the old ones and the modern ones – I especially like the contrasts here."

Miroslaw Meir Lisserman

Ukraine | Westend

Die 100-jährige Westend-Synagoge hat als einzige in Frankfurt die Novemberpogrome im Jahr 1938 überlebt. Miroslaw Meir Lisserman kennt sie von seiner Kindheit an, hat aber erst mit zunehmendem Alter den Weg zur Spiritualität gefunden.
„Wenn es geht, komme ich drei Mal täglich hierher. Wir lesen im Talmud, beten und diskutieren über die alltäglichen Gesetze des Lebens. Es gibt keine Tabus und jede Frage darf gestellt werden. Was nicht bedeutet, dass es auf jede Frage eine Antwort gibt."

Ukraine | Westend

This 100-year-old synagogue at Westend is the only one in Frankfurt, which survived the Pogroms in November 1938. Miroslaw Meir Lisserman has known the synagogue since he was a child, but has only discovered his own spirituality with his progressive age. "If possible I come here three times a day. We read the Talmud, pray and discuss the principles of daily life. There are no taboos and you can ask any question you like. Of course this doesn't mean that there is an answer to every question."

Rhodora Schorr

Philippinen | Hauptwache
„Frankfurt ist in meinen Augen wunderschön: die Hochhäuser, die vielen Menschen aus allen Teilen der Welt, die Museen und der Fluss. Vor allem die Hochhäuser im Zentrum mag ich. Und obwohl ich Frankfurt wunderbar finde, hängt mein Herz noch immer zwischen zwei Ländern. Das tut mir weh und macht mein Leben hier manchmal sehr schwierig."

The Philippines | Hauptwache
"In my opinion Frankfurt is absolutely beautiful: the skyscrapers, the many people from all over the world, the museums and the river. I particularly like the high-rise buildings in the city centre. And although I really like Frankfurt my heart is torn between two countries. That hurts and sometimes makes my life miserable."

Sivani Sivarajah

Sri Lanka | Gallus

„Ich lebe schon seit meiner Kindheit in Deutschland. Seit zwei Jahren wohne ich in Nähe der Mainzer Landstraße, was nur wenige Minuten von meiner Arbeit entfernt ist. Mein hinduistischer Sari ist in Sri Lanka Alltagskleidung, wohingegen wir uns in Deutschland so nur bei Feierlichkeiten und Hochzeiten kleiden. In Frankfurt gehe ich sowohl in den Tempel als auch in die Kirche, denn unsere Religion lässt dies zu."

Sri Lanka | Gallus

"I have been living in Germany since childhood. 2 years ago I moved close to Mainzer Landstrasse only a few minutes from where I work. In Sri Lanka my Hindi Sari is an everyday kind of dress, whereas in Germany we only wear it for weddings or festivities. In Frankfurt I go to the temple as well as to the church because our religion allows that."

Yuki Ishikawa

Japan | Kalbach

Yuki Ishikawa begreift Taiko, das Trommeln, als Sport. Diese Kleidung trägt sie bei Auftritten. Die Trommeln hat sie heute jedoch im Dojo gelassen, im Trainingsraum.

„Hier in Kalbach wohne ich zwar eher am Stadtrand, aber das stört mich nicht. Es tut gut, diese Ruhe zu haben, die Leute sind freundlich und man ist schnell im Zentrum."

Japan | Kalbach

For Yuki Ishikawa Taiko, playing the traditional Japanese drums, is like playing sport. She wears this outfit when she has a show. Today she has left her drums in the dojo, the training hall.

"Here in Kalbach we are on the outskirts of the city. I don't mind because the people are friendly and I enjoy the peace and quiet. Besides, it doesn't take long to commute into the city."

Nasim Ghadimi

Iran | Nordend

Nach der Flucht aus dem Iran hat sich Nasim Ghadimi in ihrer Kindheit vom eigenen Land abgewendet. Heute kämpft sie für mehr Freiheiten im Iran.
„Immer noch dürfen Frauen nicht öffentlich tanzen, nicht Theater spielen, nicht alleine auf der Bühne singen. Iranische Restaurants, wie auch die „Pistazie" hier im Nordend, haben all diese typisch iranischen, schönen Accessoires, die mich an die Heimat erinnern."

Iran | Nordend

After her escape from Iran as a child Nasim Ghadimi has turned her back on her own country. Today she fights for more freedom in Iran. "Women are still forbidden to dance in public, to act or sing on stage on their own. Iranian restaurants, like this one here in Nordend ("Pistazie"), have all these lovely, typically Iranian accessories which remind me of my home country."

Adriana Roselinda Sitepu-Valk

Indonesien, Nordsumatra | Zoologischer Garten
Indonesien hat mehr als 17.000 Inseln mit vielen Nationalparks und Zoos. Adriana Roselinda Sitepu-Valk zeigt sich im festlichen Kostüm, dem sogenannten Batak Karo.
„Mir gefällt, dass der Frankfurter Zoo mitten in der Stadt liegt. Hier ist es auch schön, weil alle Tiere gesund sind und gut gepflegt und man sich sicher fühlen kann. In den kleinen Zoos Indonesiens ist das leider nicht immer so."

Indonisia, North Sumatra | Zoo
Indonisia consists of more than 17.000 islands and has many national parks and zoos. Adriana Roselinda Sitepu-Valk presents herself in a festive costume, the so-called Batak Karo. "I really like the fact that the Frankfurt Zoo is right in the middle of the city. I enjoy coming here because all the animals look healthy and well taken care of. Unfortunately, that's not always the case in the small zoos in Indonesia."

81

Martin Petrus

Spanien, Katalonien | Campus Westend

„Wenn ich nach meiner Identität gefragt werde, antworte ich immer, dass ich zweieinhalb Identitäten habe – nämlich eine Mixtur aus deutscher, spanischer und katalanischer."
In Frankfurt und Barcelona aufgewachsen, fühlt sich Martin Petrus auch im Haus Baskischer Studien heimisch, einem Institut, das er mit aufgebaut hat und heute koordiniert. Er trägt hier das typisch baskische rote Halstuch und die Txapela, die Baskenmütze.

Spain, Catalonia | Campus Westend

"When people ask me what nationality I have, I always answer that I have got two and a half – that is a blend of German, Spanish and Catalan." Having grown up in both countries, namely Barcelona and Frankfurt, Martin Petrus also feels at home at the House of Basque Studies, an institute he helped setting up and which he manages today. On this photo he wears the typical Basque scarf and the Txapela, a beret or hat.

Didi Sudesh Sethi

Indien | Eschersheim
Didi Sudesh Sethi trägt immer weiße Kleidung, um äußere und innere Reinheit und Schlichtheit zu zeigen und auch, um morgens keine Gedanken über die Farbwahl verschwenden zu müssen. Wenn sie in Frankfurt ist, verbringt sie die meiste Zeit im Raja Yoga Zentrum am Weißen Stein.
„Hier erlebe ich mein wahres Ich in Harmonie mit meinem inneren Sein und in Beziehung mit all denjenigen, die sich hier ebenso aufhalten und auf der Suche nach sich und nach Respekt vor sich selbst sind."

India | Eschersheim
Didi Sudesh Sethi always wears the colour white. It reflects inner as well as outer cleanliness and simplicity and avoids spending a lot of time on choosing what colour to wear in the morning. When she is in Frankfurt she is to be found at Raja Yoga Centre at Weißer Stein. "Here I experience my true self in harmony with my inner being and with all those who are in search of their self and respect for themselves."

Jelena Katanovic

Bosnien | Sachsenhausen

In dem serbischen Kostüm tanzt Jelena Katanovic in ganz Europa mit ihrem Verein, der sich auch humanitär für Bosnien und Serbien engagiert.

„Eigentlich bin ich Serbin. Aber meine Eltern lebten in Bosnien, deshalb habe ich auch den bosnischen Pass. Ich bin aber in Frankfurt geboren und lebe schon immer in Sachsenhausen. Hier habe ich meine Freundinnen und Freunde. In Bosnien meine Familie."

Bosnia | Sachsenhausen

When Jelena Katanovic is dancing all over Europe with her organization she wears this Serbian costume. This organization is also committed to humanitarian causes in Bosnia and Serbia. "Actually, I am Serbian, but my parents have lived in Bosnia. That's why I also have a Bosnian passport. I was born in Frankfurt however, and have always lived in Sachsenhausen. All my friends live here; my family lives in Bosnia."

Rogerio Gomez

Brasilien | Alt Sachsenhausen

„Als ich vor fünf Jahren nach Frankfurt gekommen bin, hat mein Leben neu angefangen. Ich habe Deutsch gelernt und viele Leute getroffen. Wir tanzen zusammen – nicht nur ecuadorianische Volkstänze, Salsa, Bachata und Merengue, sondern auch Tänze der Indianer aus dem Amazonas. Meine Oma war Indianerin, deshalb interessiert mich die indianische Kultur. Ich tanze in Frankfurt, mein Leben ist jetzt hier."

Brazil | Alt Sachsenhausen

"When I came to Frankfurt 5 years ago my life started anew. I learned German and met many people. We dance together – not just Ecuadorian folk dances, but also salsa, bachata and merengue as well as dances from the indigenous people of the Amazon. Since my grandma was a native, I am interested in indigenous culture. Now I dance in Frankfurt, my life is here."

Claudia Tonantzin Mandujano Ortiz

Mexiko | Bornheim

„Als ich im Jahr 2000 zum ersten Mal nach Frankfurt kam, wohnte ich in Bornheim. Ständig verlief ich mich in den Gassen. Meine Deutschlehrer hatten mir ein sehr höfliches Deutsch beigebracht. Nur: Wenn ich endlich mein einleitendes 'Entschuldigen Sie bitte die Störung' herausgebracht hatte, um nach dem Weg zu fragen, waren die Angesprochenen auch schon weg. Immer kam ich zu diesem Lokal, von dem aus ich die Straßen ablief, um zurück nach Hause zu finden."

Mexico | Bornheim

"When I came to Frankfurt for the first time in the year 2000, I lived in Bornheim. I got lost regularly in the alleyways. My German teachers had taught me very polite German. The problem was that the people I asked for the way had already gone by the time I had said:
"Excuse me, please, may I ask for your help". I always went to that one pub from which I walked down the streets to find the way back home."

Mayte Vega

Ecuador | Nizza am Mainufer

Mayte Vega lebt schon länger in Frankfurt am Main, als sie jemals in Ecuador gelebt hat. Das folkloristische Oberteil aus Otavalo ist handbestickt und gehörte ihrer Großmutter.
„Das ist ein sehr gemütlicher Platz zum Picknicken, aber auch zum Feiern. Außerdem hatte ich mit meiner Tanzgruppe bereits mehrere Auftritte am Mainufer."

Ecuador | Nizza at the bank of the river Main

Mayte Vega has already lived much longer in Frankfurt than she has ever lived in Ecuador. Her folk top from Otavalo is handmade and belonged to her grandmother. "This is a perfect place for picnics and parties. Besides, I have already had several gigs with my dance group here."

Rokeya Sultana-Rothe

Bangladesh | Ginnheimer Spargel
„Im Sommer komme ich jeden Tag in meinen kleinen Garten in der Schrebergartenkolonie am Ginnheimer Spargel, egal, welches Wetter gerade ist. Ich habe Samen aus meiner Heimat mitgebracht, und so züchte ich Kräuter und Gemüse heran, die ich in Deutschland nicht finden konnte. Wir sind hier wie eine kleine Dorfgemeinschaft und meine Nachbarn kommen aus fast allen Ländern der Welt."

Bangladesh | Ginnheimer Spargel
"In the summer I go to my allotment at Ginnheimer Spargel every day regardless of the weather. I have brought seeds from my hometown so I can grow herbs and vegetables I can't find in Germany. We are just like a village community, my neighbours, who are almost from all over the world, and I."

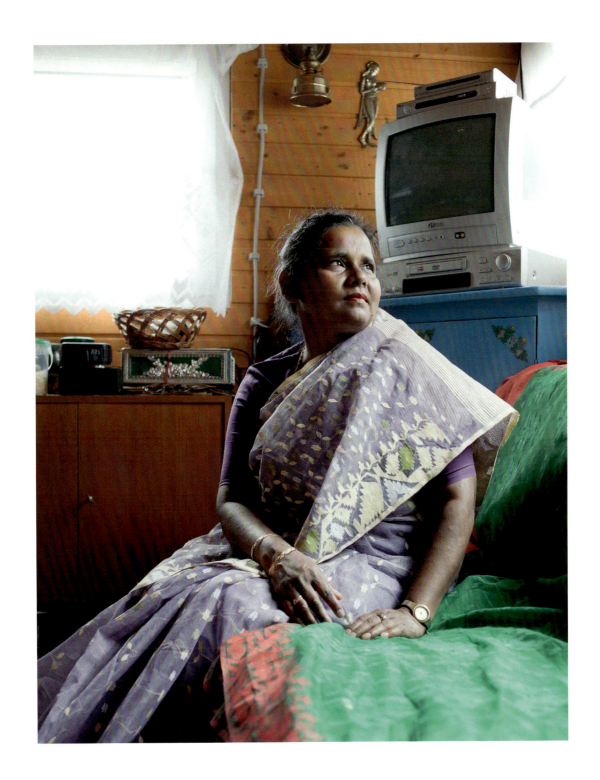

Carlos Carralero

Kuba | Innenstadt
„Mit der kleinen Zigarrenmanufaktur, die ich zusammen mit meiner Freundin hier aufgebaut habe, setze ich eine Familientradition fort. Meine Großmutter arbeitete auf Kuba in einer Zigarrenmanufaktur. Die Familie von meiner Freundin besitzt Tabakplantagen in der Dominikanischen Republik. Zigarren gehören zu meiner Kultur. Sie herzustellen, ist eine Kunst, die viel an Liebe und Geduld bedarf. Beides habe ich nach Frankfurt mitgebracht."

Cuba | City Centre
"I follow a family tradition with my hand-made cigars which I produce together with my girlfriend. My grandmother used to work in a cigar factory in Cuba. My girlfriend's family owns a tobacco plantation in the Dominican Republic. Cigars are part of my culture. It takes a lot of skill and patience to make them. I have brought both to Frankfurt."

Maria Betania Arcanjo Köhler

Brasilien | Hausen

„Mir ist es wichtig, etwas Ursprüngliches aus Brasilien zu zeigen. Es sollte eine Kleidung der Indios sein. Der Stamm war für mich dabei nicht so entscheidend. Die Brotfabrik ist ein Kulturzentrum, in dem sich verschiedene Nationen treffen und etwas präsentieren. Das ist genau wie bei unserer Tanzgruppe, in der nicht nur Brasilianer auftreten, sondern Menschen aus allen Ländern. Das bedeutet für mich Integration."

Brazil | Hausen

"To me it's important to show something authentic from Brazil. I wanted it to be clothes worn by the indigenous people. The tribe was not so important to me. The Brotfabrik is an arts centre where different people meet and present something. That's exactly like our dance group, which doesn't consist of Brazilians only, but of people from different countries. And that's what integration means to me."

Van Tu Uyen

Vietnam | Innenstadt

Obwohl erst 21 Jahre alt und noch nicht verheiratet, trägt Van Tu Uyen ein königsblaues Hochzeitskleid, auf dem in alt-vietnamesischer Schrift „100 Jahre Glück" steht.

„Das Kleid habe ich von meiner Tante geliehen. In Vietnam hatten wir kein Glück. Wir mussten flüchten und sind nach Frankfurt gekommen. Ich lebe sehr gerne hier. Auch zum Studieren will ich nicht weggehen. Die ‚Bonsai Lounge' ist der perfekte Treffpunkt für vietnamesische Jugendliche mitten in der Stadt."

Vietnam | City Centre

Although just 21 years old and not yet married, Van Tu Uyen wears a wedding gown in royal blue. "100 lucky years" is stiched on it in old Vietnamese letters. "I borrowed the gown from my aunt. In Vietnam we weren't lucky. We had to escape and came to Frankfurt. I am really happy here and also plan to go to the local university. "Bonsai Lounge" is a perfect meeting place for Vietnamese youngsters right in the middle of the city."

Barbara und Thomas Hentschl

Österreich und Deutschland | Palmengarten

Die Iseltaler Tracht, die Barbara und Thomas Hentschl im Palmengarten tragen, sieht man normalerweise eher auf Tiroler Festen. „Der Palmengarten ist ein Stück Natur in der Stadt. Wir lieben das Grüne und die Vielfalt der Pflanzen und es gibt tolle Ausstellungen. Auch mit den Kindern kommen wir oft hierher."

Austria and Germany | Palmengarten

You would normally see the Iseltaler traditional gown, that Barbara und Thomas Hentschl are wearing in the Palmengarten, on festivals in Tyrol. "The Palmengarten represents nature in the city. We love the greenery and the diversity of the plants. There are also great exhibitions. We also take our children here quite often."

Agnieszka Łopuszńska-Krüger

Polen | Willy-Brandt-Platz

In ihrer Krakauer Tracht ist Agnieszka Łopuszńska-Krüger oft bei Tanz- und Gesangsauftritten im ganzen Rhein-Main-Gebiet unterwegs.

„Da ich aus der Provinz komme, hat Frankfurt mich einerseits sehr fasziniert, zugleich aber auch eingeschüchtert. Genauso empfinde ich diesen starken Kontrast an dem Ort, den ich ausgesucht habe. Meine bunte, freudige, temperamentvolle Tracht vor der grauen, eckigen und kalten Treppe inmitten der Stadt."

Poland | Willy-Brandt-Platz

Agnieszka Łopuszńska-Krüger often wears her Krakow costume at dance performances throughout the Rhein-Main-Area. "Coming from a rural area I was absolutely fascinated by Frankfurt and at the same time intimidated. I feel the same strong contrast at this place I have chosen: my spirited, colourful, happy costume against the grey, squared and cold stairs in the middle of the city."

Amir Mansoor

Pakistan | Bahnhofsviertel

Amir Mansoor trägt die pakistanische Kleidung, ein Karachi, eigentlich nur dann, wenn er zur Moschee in der Münchner Straße geht. Er liebt die Hektik dieses Viertels sowie die pakistanischen Köstlichkeiten seines dortigen Lieblingsrestaurants. Der Reiseverkehrskaufmann ist auch Schauspieler, Regisseur und Tänzer.
„Ich bewundere die Ordnung, das strukturelle Denken und die Pünktlichkeit der Deutschen. Nur schade, dass ich hier nicht, wie in Pakistan, meine Brötchen im Pyjama holen kann."

Pakistan | Bahnhofsviertel

Amir Mansoor actually only wears Pakistani clothes, the so-called Karachi, when he goes to Mosque in Münchner Strasse. He loves the hustle and bustle of this part of town just like the Pakistani delicacies in his favourite restaurant there. He not only works in tourism he is also an actor, director and dancer. "I really admire the Germans' sense of order, their structural thinking and punctuality. I only regret that it's not possible to go to the bakery for rolls in a pyjama like in Pakistan."

Vanesa Piña Sánchez

Spanien | Höchst

„Ich bin in Höchst geboren und gehe hier zur Schule. Auch unser Flamencoverein ist in diesem Stadtteil Frankfurts. Da tanze ich, seit ich drei Jahre alt bin. Mittlerweile unterrichte ich mit einer Freundin die Kleinen. Die Sommerferien verbringe ich immer in Spanien. Beide Länder gehören zu mir. In keinem fühle ich mich fremd. Im Sommer feiern wir hier das Höchster Schlossfest. Das ist etwas ganz Besonderes, denn dort mischt sich alles; alle feiern zusammen und haben Spaß."

Spain | Höchst

"I was born in Höchst and go to school here. Our flamenco club is also in this part of the city. I have been dancing the flamenco since I was 3 years old. Now I am teaching the young ones together with my friend. I always spend my summer holidays in Spain. Both countries belong to me. They are both familiar to me. In the summer we celebrate the Höchster Schlossfest here. That's something very special because everyone gets together there. We all celebrate together and enjoy ourselves."

Xiaojun Liu

China | Ostpark

Xiaojun Liu trägt im Ostpark das festliche chinesische Kostüm Qipao.

„Ich kenne den Park schon lange. Das erste Mal waren wir im Zirkus am Ratswegplatz gegenüber. Da haben wir den Park entdeckt. Wir grillen hier manchmal Garnelen und Fisch – eher die leichte Kost."

China | Ostpark

Xiaojun Liu wears her festive Chinese costume, the Qipao, at Ostpark. "I have known the park for a long time. The first time we went to a circus on Ratsweg just on the other side of the street. Sometimes we barbecue prawns and fish here – rather light food."

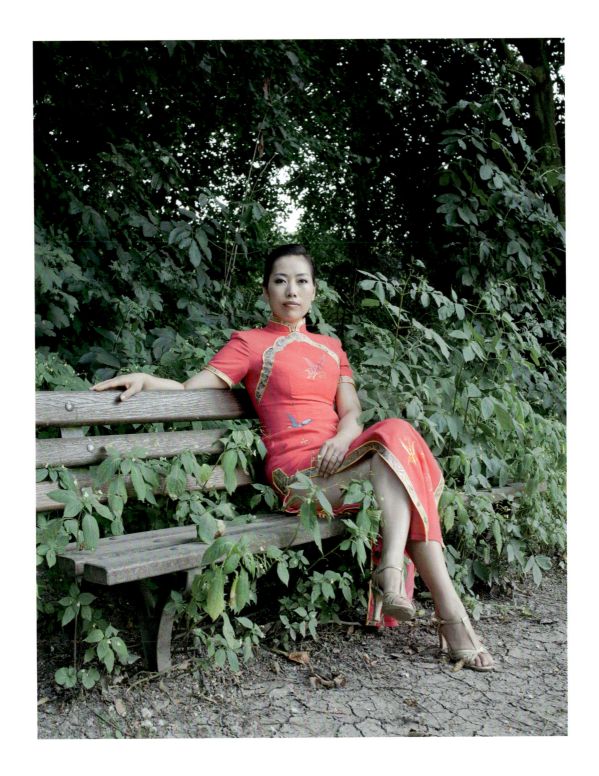

Hafizur Rahman und Abul Amanullah

Bangladesh | Mertonviertel

„Ich lebe gerne im Mertonviertel", sagt Abul Amanullah. „Mir gefällt, dass ich schnell in der Natur bin. Im Sommer gehe ich fast jeden Tag in den Niddawiesen spazieren. Überhaupt erinnert mich das Wasser von Nidda und Urselbach an mein flussreiches Heimatland. Wenn ich morgens zur Arbeit gehe, komme ich immer an einem Kindergarten vorbei, in dem Kinder aus den unterschiedlichsten Kulturen miteinander spielen. Dann fühle ich, dass Frankfurt meine neue Heimat ist."

Bangladesh | Mertonviertel

"I like to live in this area also because the countryside is so close by. In the summertime, I go for walks along the river Nidda almost every day. I realize how much the water from the Nidda and the Urselbach remind me of my home country, which has many rivers. When I go to work in the morning, I always pass a nursery school where I see children from all kinds of cultures playing together. That's when I feel that Frankfurt has become my new home."

Dasitu Kajela-Röttger

Äthiopien, Oromo | Am Holbeinsteg
„Flüsse begleiten mich seit meiner Kindheit, sie tragen auch Geschichten mit sich. Daher war es ganz klar, dass ich mich am Museumsufer fotografieren lassen wollte. Der Main hat mir viel gegeben – ohne ihn hätte ich die Sehnsucht nach meiner Heimat weniger gut überwunden. Er trägt Lebensfreude in die Stadt und birgt noch eine Ursprünglichkeit der Landschaft in sich. Er schenkt der Stadt Natur."

Ethiopia, Oromo | At Holbeinsteg
"Since childhood rivers have been part of my life. They also carry stories. That's why I had to have my picture taken at the river. The river Main has given me a lot – without it I wouldn't have been able to overcome my longing for my hometown. It is like he carries joy for life into the city and reveals nature in its purest form. He gives that gift to the city – nature."

Olga Denisova

Weißrussland | Gutleut

„Ich mag Frankfurt! Vor allem die Gegensätze: Von der Industrielandschaft zur Altstadt, vom Bänker zum Musiker, von der Autobahn zur engen Gasse – alles passt wie durch ein Wunder in diese kompakte Stadt hinein. Mir gefällt die Atmosphäre von Industriebauten. Es ist ein kleiner Nervenkitzel, sich an solchen Orten aufzuhalten: Sie wirken so kalt und leer, aber wenn man sich einmal hineingetraut hat, sind sie spannend und aufregend."

Belarus | Gutleut

"I like Frankfurt! Mainly the contrasts: From the industrial landscape to the old town, from the banker to the musician, from the motorway to the alleys – mysteriously, everything fits into this very compact city. I particularly like the atmosphere of the industrial buildings. It's somehow exciting to spend time at those places: they seem cold and empty at first, but when you have ventured inside you realise how fascinating they really are."

Joaquina und Manuel Costa

Portugal | Bockenheim

Joaquina und Manuel Costa lassen sich an der Bockenheimer Warte gemeinsam fotografieren, denn nur zu zweit ist für sie die portugiesische Tracht komplett.

„Schade, dass die Studenten aus diesem Stadtteil bald alle weg sein werden. Das hat viel Leben hierher gebracht. Wir bleiben. Wir leben schon seit 25 Jahren in Bockenheim."

Portugal | Bockenheim

Joaquina and Manuel Costa had their photo taken together at Bockenheimer Warte. Only in pairs is the Portugese costume complete. "It is a pity that the students in this part of the city soon all will be gone. They were very stimulating. We will stay. We have been living in Bockenheim for 25 years."

Laila Bouhadou

Marokko | Bahnhofsviertel

Laila Bouhadou trägt einen marokkanischen Kaftan, der für sie in Marokko genäht wurde.

„Das Bahnhofsviertel ist der 'Melting Pot' – ein Viertel, in dem sich das internationale Leben abspielt. Ich gehe total gern dort einkaufen: Lebensmittel, Stoffe, Süßigkeiten und Gebäck – es gibt alles. Für mich gibt es keine Alternative zu Frankfurt. Ich liebe diese Stadt."

Morocco | Bahnhofsviertel

Laila Bouhadou wears a Moroccan caftan which was made for her in Morocco. "This part of town is the "melting pot" - a district buzzing with international life. I simply love to shop here: food, fabrics, sweets and pastries – you find everything. There is no alternative to Frankfurt in my opinion. I love this city."

Feng-Ming Wudy

Taiwan | Alter Flugplatz

Auf dem ehemaligen Militärflugplatz in Frankfurt Bonames landen und starten schon längst keine Flugzeuge mehr. Feng-Ming Wudy genießt die frische Luft in ihrem traditionellen chinesischen Kostüm.

„Mein Mann und ich spazieren hier öfters oder trinken Kaffee. Für unseren Hund ist es auch schön, denn der darf frei herumlaufen und muss nicht an der Leine gehen. Der alte Flugplatz ist ein Ort, an dem ich mich gelassen fühle."

Taiwan | Old Airfield

It's a long time since airplanes have taken off from or landed on this former military airfield in Frankfurt Bonames. Feng-Ming Wudy enjoys the fresh air. She is wearing her traditional Chinese costume. "My husband and I often go for a walk or have a cup of coffee here. Our dog also likes it, because he can run around freely and doesn't have to be on a lead. The Old Airfield is a place where I feel calm."

Eleonora Judschenko

Russland, Sibirien | Nordend

Wenn sie die Bretter dieser Welt in ihrer sibirischen Tracht oder mit ihrer russischen Theatergruppe nicht erklimmt, zieht sich die 14-jährige Eleonora Judschenko manchmal auf dieses Dach am Baumweg zurück, wo sie die Stille und Einsamkeit genießt. „Wenn ich früher meine sibirische Geburtsstadt verlassen habe, habe ich jedes Mal geweint. Heute nicht mehr. In Frankfurt bin ich zu Hause. Auch die Schule macht mir hier viel mehr Spaß."

Russia, Siberia | Nordend

When she is not performing in her Siberian traditional gown or acting with her Russian theater group, 14-year-old Eleonora Judschenko sometimes withdraws to this rooftop on Baumweg to enjoy the quiet and solitude. "In the past, whenever I left my hometown, I always cried. Not anymore today. In Frankfurt I feel at home. I also enjoy school much more here."

Paratikchya und Samikchhya Pokhrel

Nepal | Nordweststadt
Paratikchya Pokhrel trägt das sommerliche Chhit Ko Sari & Choli und ihre Schwester Samikchhya das geschlossene Gurung – beides Kostüme, die heute nur noch bei Tanzauftritten getragen werden. „Im Titus-Forum des Saalbaus im Nordwestzentrum hat meine Schwester mit ihrer Schule Abschluss gefeiert. Hier wollten wir fotografiert werden, denn wir fanden die Atmosphäre, die Leuchter und die Bühne toll. Nun besuchen wir die Fachhochschule. Samikchhya ist besser in Englisch. Ich in Mathe."

Nepal | Nordweststadt
Paratikchya Pokhrel wears the summer-like Chhit Ko Sari & Choli and her sister Samikchhya the closed Gurung. Today both costumes are only worn at performances. "My sister had her graduation ceremony in the Titus-Forum at Nordwestzentrum. We wanted our pictures taken right here because we really liked the atmosphere, the chandeliers and the stage. Now we go to the technical college. Samikchhya is better at English. I am better at maths."

Über die Fotografin Anna Pekala

Anna Pekala möchte unterwegs sein, auf Reisen, aber auch zu Hause. Das verlangt eine innere Haltung: offen bleiben für neue Eindrücke, andere Menschen und ihre Lebensweisen. Dabei ist ihre Kamera das Mittel, sich Welten zu erschließen und Eindrücke festzuhalten.

Für dieses Buch hat Anna Pekala fünfzig Menschen portraitiert. Während der Aufnahmen entsteht plötzlich eine fast intime Situation zwischen zwei Fremden. Im Spannungsfeld zwischen sich zeigen und gesehen werden kommunizieren Fotografin und Modell miteinander. Die portraitierten Menschen spielen hier keine vorgegebene Rolle, sondern stellen sich selbst und ihre Kultur dar.

Durch den Ausschnitt des Suchers betrachtet, schrumpft die weite Welt zusammen. Es ist Anna Pekalas Blick, der auswählt und eine Ordnung zwischen den Dingen sucht. Später wird das Foto hingegen ein Ganzes sein, ein Kosmos, in dem die Menschen und Dinge eine neue Bedeutung erhalten: In der Südseekulisse eines Innenhofes wird ein zufälliger Fleck auf dem Boden zu einer Welle. Verschiedene Bildelemente finden zusammen oder bilden einen Kontrast – die Kopfbedeckung und das Muster des Bodens, das rot-weiß-blaue Kleid und die Verkehrszeichen. Anna Pekalas Fotografien bergen Geschichten, die von uns weitererzählt werden.

Anna Pekala, geboren 1979 in Wodzislaw Śląski in Polen, lebt seit ihrem elften Lebensjahr in Deutschland. Während ihres Studiums in der HfG Offenbach bei Prof. Frank Schumacher und Prof. Martin Liebscher entwickelte sich ihr thematischer Schwerpunkt. In ihren Projekten fotografiert sie Menschen in ihrer Umgebung. Unter Anderem besuchte sie Sinti- und Roma-Familien, die Bewohner eines beskidischen Dorfes und Transylvaniens.

Katja Piontek

About the photographer Anna Pekala

Anna Pekala likes to travel as much as she enjoys staying at home. Therefore, she has established a certain attitude: To be open towards new impressions, other people and their way of life. Her medium is the photo camera to exploit her surroundings and to capture impressions.

She portrayed 50 people for this book. During the photo shoots, it is as if the photographer and the object get caught up in an intimate situation. They communicate with each other surrounded by tension. A tension based on being exposed and watched. Here, the people portrayed are not playing a given role. They purely represent themselves and their culture.

The wide world shrinks through a cutout of the seeker's eye. Anna Pekala's selective view searches amongst objects for arrangements. These arrangements will become whole again in one single image. Like a cosmos where people and objects obtain a new meaning: At the South Sea backdrop of a courtyard a random spot on the ground turns into a wave. Different picture elements conform or turn to a contrast, for example the headdress and the pattern on the ground or the red-white-blue coloured dress and the road signs. Within her photographs you can discover stories, which we continue telling.

Anna Pekala was born 1979 in Wodzislaw Śląski, Poland. She lives in Germany since she was eleven years old. During her studies at HfG Offenbach under Prof. Frank Schumacher and Prof. Martin Liebscher she emphasized on her main subject of interest. These are projects about people, whom she photographed in their surroundings. Amongst others, she visited Sinti and Romani families, which are habitants of Beskidish villages and Transylvanians.

Katja Piontek

Die Portraitierten und ihre Vereine
Portrayed people and their associations

Seite / Page	Name	Verein, Institution / Association, Institution
28	Emilia Flügel	Malaysian Club Deutschland e. V. / Malaysian Club Germany e. V.
30	Jean Jules Tatchouop	Deutsch-Kamerunische Gesellschaft e. V. / German-Cameroonian Association e. V.
32	Monika Banasova	Deutsch-Slowakischer Kulturklub Frankfurt e. V. / German-Slovakian Cultural Club Frankfurt e. V.
34	Georgina Mercedes Reyes	SonTaino
36	Ismat El-Turk, Usama Sabih	Jordanisch-Irakischer Freundschaftsverein e. V. / Jordanian-Iraqi Friendship Association e. V.
38	Mariam Mwabasi	Maweni e. V.
40	Elsa Nava Villarroel	Puerta del Sol e. V.
42	Grigorios Zarcadas	Griechische Gemeinde e. V. / Greek Congregation e. V.
44	Nino Kambegashvili	Musikschule Goldene Taste / Golden Key Music School
46	Giovanni Belenzano	AFI Verein italienischer Familien e. V. / AFI Association of Italian Families e. V.
48	Fabiana Jarma	academia de tango / Tango Academy
50	Halil Özdemir	Alevitische Gemeinde Frankfurt e. V. / Alevism Congregation Frankfurt e. V.
52	Ho-Jeong Reinbacher	Koreanische Tanzgruppe / Korean Dance Group
54	Bertrand Caradec	OuverTüre e. V.

56	Sandra Jiliana Peña Burgos	Deutsch-Kolumbianischer Verein e. V.
		German-Columbian Association e. V.
58	Abderrahim Bouzaidi	DMK Deutsch-Marokkanisches Kompetenznetzwerk e. V.
		DMK German-Maroccan Network of Excellence e. V.
60	Ranto Harilala Schlosser	Madagaskar Gruppe e. V.
		Madagascar Group e. V.
62	Constanta Danilovic	Paul-Hindemith-Schule
		Paul-Hindemith-School
64	Agassi Bangura	Sierra Leonisch-Deutscher Freundschaftsverein e. V.
		Sierra Leone – German Friendship Association e. V.
66	Sunny Graff	Frauen in Bewegung Taekwondo und Selbstverteidigung e. V.
		Women in Action Taekwondo and Self Defense e. V.
68	Tyagita Hidayat und Mahar Muhammad	Nusa Irama e. V.
70	Miroslaw Meir Lisserman	Jewish Experience e. V.
72	Rhodora Schorr	Philippinisches Kulturinstitut e. V.
		Philippine Cultural Institute e. V.
74	Sivani Sivarajah	Tamilische Schule
		Tamil School
76	Yuki Ishikawa	Kurinoki Wadaiko Frankfurt
78	Nasim Ghadimi	Freiheit für Iran e. V.
		Freedom for Iran e. V.
80	Adriana Roselinda Sitepu-Valk	Permif e. V.
82	Martin Petrus	Haus Baskischer Studien, Goethe-Universität
		House of Basque Studies, Goethe-University
84	Didi Sudesh Sethi	Raja Yoga Institut
86	Jelena Katanovic	Kultur- und humanitärer Verein „KOLO" e. V.
		Culture and Humanitarian Association „KOLO" e. V.

88	Rogerio Gomez	Südamerikanische Tanzgruppe Juyana
		South American Dance Group Juyana
90	Claudia Tonantzin Mandujano Ortiz	OuverTüre e. V.
92	Mayte Vega	Juyana Tanzgruppe
		Juyana Dance Group
94	Rokeya Sultana-Rothe	Freundschaft und Fortschritt e. V.
		Friendship and Progress e. V.
96	Carlos Carralero	Kubanische Gruppe
		Cuban Group
98	Maria Betania Arcanjo Köhler	Brasilianischer Kulturverein Guarani e. V.
		Brazilian Cultural Club Guarani e. V.
100	Van Tu Uyen	Verein der vietnamesischen Flüchtlinge in Frankfurt und Umgebung e. V.
		Association of Vietnamese Refugees in Frankfurt and Surroundings e. V.
102	Barbara und Thomas Hentschl	Polyhymnia Offenbach & Blasorchester Heusenstamm
		Polyhymnia Offenbach & Brass Orchestra Heusenstamm
104	Agnieszka Łopuszńska-Krüger	Deutsch-Polnischer Kulturverein SALONik e. V. & Folkloreverein Krakowiak
		German-Polish Cultural Club SALONik e. V. & Folklore Club Krakowiak
106	Amir Mansoor	Pakbann Theater e. V.
108	Vanesa Piña Sánchez	Peña Flamenca los Cabales e. V.
110	Xiaojun Liu	Chinesische Sprachenschule Huayin
		Chinese Language School Huayin
112	Hafizur Rahman und Abul Amanullah	Main Bildungs- und Integrationsforum (mabin) e. V.
		Education and Integration Forum Main (mabin) e. V.
114	Dasitu Kajela-Röttger	Oromo Hilfsinitiative e. V., Frankfurt
		Oromo Aid Initiative e. V., Frankfurt
116	Olga Denisova	Capoeira Jacobina Arte

118	Joaquina und Manuel Costa	Portugiesisches Kulturzentrum e. V.
		Portuguese Cultural Centre e. V.
120	Laila Bouhadou	Osten trifft auf Westen e. V.
		Orient meets Occident e. V.
122	Feng-Ming Wudy	Deutsch-Taiwanesischer Frauenverein e. V.
		German-Taiwanese Women's Association e. V.
124	Eleonora Judschenko	ISTOK e. V.
126	Paratikchya und Samikchhya Pokhrel	Nepali Samaj e. V.

Danke

Danke an alle, die sich bereit erklärt haben, sich für diesen Bildband fotografieren zu lassen und uns ihre kostbare Zeit für den Termin geschenkt haben.

Danke an alle Betreiber, Firmen und Institutionen, bei denen wir unentgeltlich die Fotos machen durften und auch das eine oder andere Mal darüber hinaus noch bewirtet wurden.

Danke an die Unterstützer dieses Projekts, dem AmkA mit Mario Will und dem Jugendbildungswerk mit Roland Sautner und Tina Bender, dem Verein OuverTüre – Deutsch-französischer Verein zur Förderung des internationalen Sprach- und Kulturaustauschs – mit Sébastien Daudin und Judith Zimmermann, die von Beginn an bei diesem Buchprojekt mitgearbeitet haben.

Danke dem Historischen Museum mit Wolf von Wolzogen und seinem Rat bei dem Rückblick auf Frankfurts Geschichte der Migration.

Danke an Florian Albrecht-Schoeck, der uns beim Layout geholfen hat sowie an Renate Aßmus für ihre geduldige Korrektur. Ein besonderer Dank gilt dem Societäts-Verlag, der uns von Beginn an das Vertrauen geschenkt hat: insbesondere an Sibylle Schmidt, die uns mit Rat und Tat bei der Erstellung des Buchs zur Seite gestanden hat, das Sie jetzt in Ihren Händen halten und in dem Sie immer wieder blättern können.

Ihr Frankfurter Jugendring
Jan Lamprecht, Vorsitzender, Turgut Yüksel, Referent/Projektkoordinator

Acknowledgements

Thanks to all who had their picture taken for this book and gave us their precious time for the photo shoots.

Thanks to all operators, companies and institutions that allowed us to develop the pictures complimentarily and for the one or other great hospitality.

Thanks to the supporters of this project Mario Will of AmkA, Roland Sautner and Tina Bender of the Jugendbildungswerk. As well as Sébastien Daudin und Judith Zimmermann of the OuverTüre which is a German-French association promoting international language and culture exchange. They were involved in this book right from the start.

Thanks to Wolf von Wolzogen of the Historische Museum and his advice on the review of Frankfurt's migration history.

Thanks to Florian Albrecht-Schoeck for the layout work and to Renate Aßmus for her patient proof-reading. As well a special thanks to the Societäts-Verlag (publisher) who trusted us right from the start: especially to Sibylle Schmidt who guided us in word and deed while constructing this book; that you may now hold in your hands and browse through it again and again.

Your Frankfurter Jugendring
Jan Lamprecht, chairman, Turgut Yüksel, coordinator

mein frankfurt und ich.
Portraits

my frankfurt and i.
Portraits

Ein Projekt von:
A project by:

Trägerverein des Frankfurter Jugendrings e. V.
Hansaallee 150
60320 Frankfurt am Main
Telefon: 069 | 56 000 1-0
www.frankfurterjugendring.de

Jugend- und Sozialamt – Jugendbildungswerk der Stadt Frankfurt am Main
Eschersheimer Landstraße 241-249
60320 Frankfurt am Main
Telefon: 069 | 212 – 38531
www.jugendbildungswerk-ffm.de/

OuverTüre e. V.
Wiesenstr. 50
60385 Frankfurt am Main
www.ouvertuere.org

Unterstützt von:
Supported by:

  *Frankfurter Programm Aktive Nachbarschaft*